Greenville

Welcome!

Photo by Studio D Photographers.

Greenville

Willkommen

Bienvenue

BENVENUTO

ようこそ

Welcome!

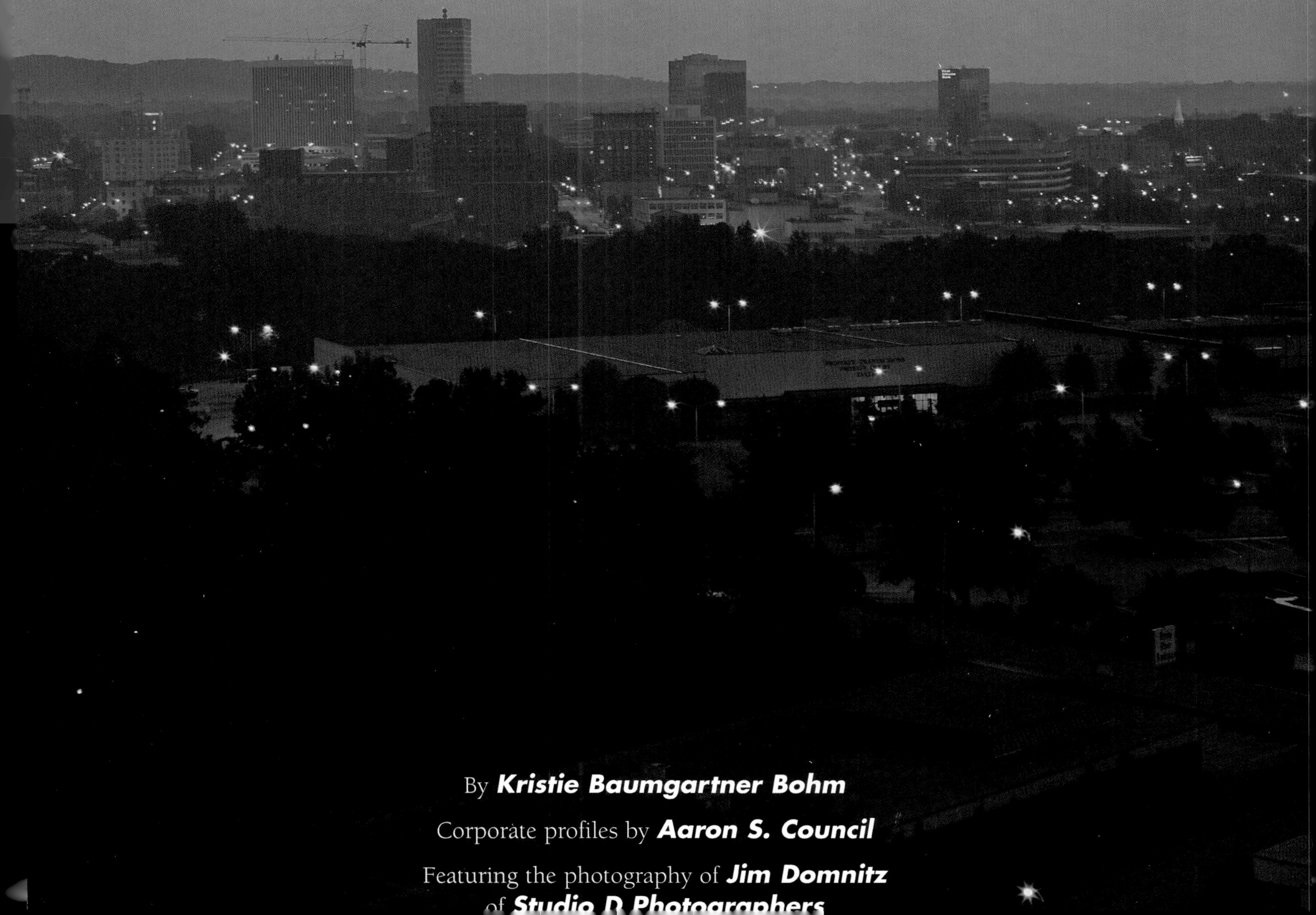

By **Kristie Baumgartner Bohm**

Corporate profiles by **Aaron S. Council**

Featuring the photography of **Jim Domnitz**
of **Studio D Photographers**

Greenville: Welcome!

Produced in cooperation with the Greater Greenville Chamber of Commerce

24 Cleveland St.
Greenville, SC 29601
(864) 242-1050

By Kristie Baumgartner Bohm
Corporate profiles by Aaron Council
Featuring the photography of Jim Domnitz of Studio D Photographers

Community Communications, Inc.
Publishers: Ronald P. Beers and James E. Turner

Staff for *Greenville: Welcome!*
Publisher's Sales Associate: John Lorenzo
Executive Editor: James E. Turner
Managing Editor: Kurt R. Niland
Profile Editor: Robin Davies
Design Director: Camille Leonard
Designer: Scott Phillips
Profile Designer: Lenita Gilreath
Photo Editors: Scott Phillips and Kurt R. Niland
Production Manager: Cindy Lovett
Editorial Assistant: Jarrod Stiff
Contract Manager: Katrina Williams
Sales Assistant: Annette R. Lozier
Accounting Services: Sara Ann Turner
Printing Production: Frank Rosenberg/GSAmerica

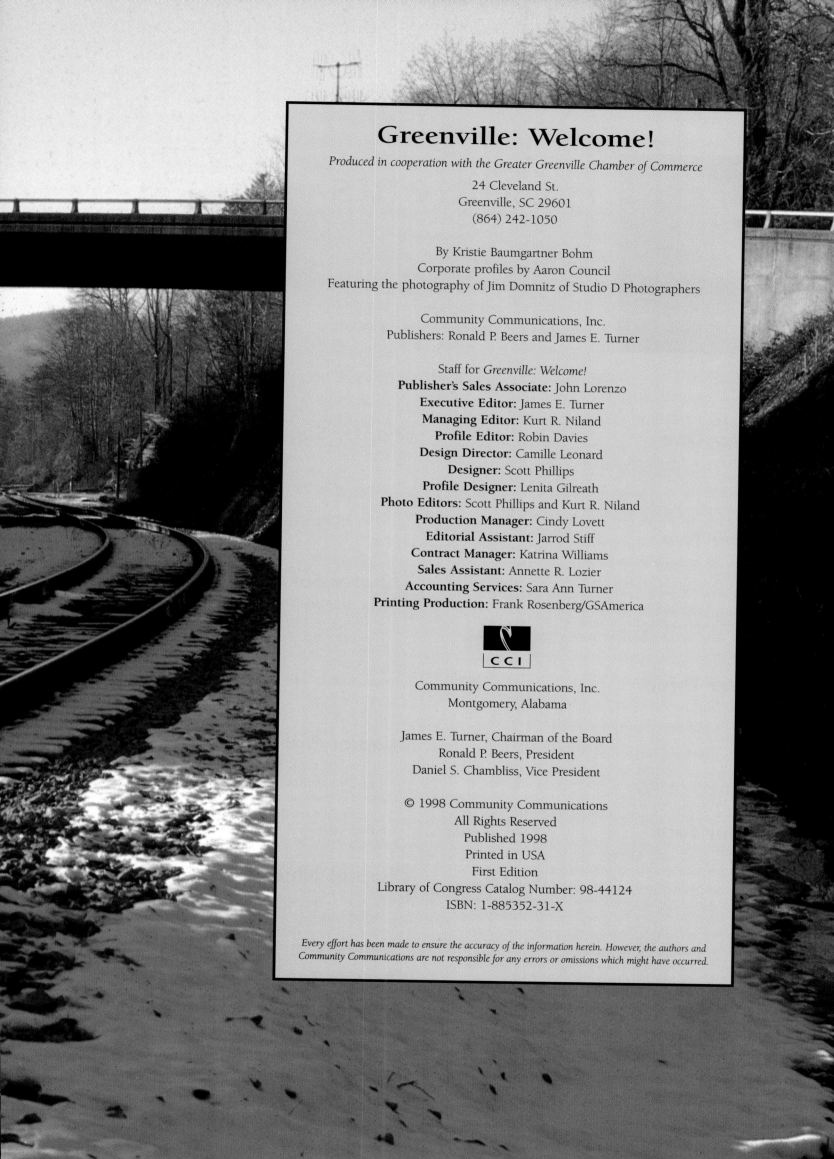

Community Communications, Inc.
Montgomery, Alabama

James E. Turner, Chairman of the Board
Ronald P. Beers, President
Daniel S. Chambliss, Vice President

Contents

Chapter One   14

Greenville: Small Town Feel, Big City Amenities

"Greenville's birthplace began near a beautiful waterfall along the banks of the Reedy River. Now more than 225 years later, that site has become the center of a thriving, prosperous international city."

Chapter Two   30

Enterprise: We're In Business

"Greenville's economic vitality reflects the community's diligence to excel at the task at hand, pursue new business opportunities, and plan for the future. The community's geographic location, hospitable people, and solid infrastructure have allowed this community to achieve distinction, attracting businesses from all over the world."

Chapter Three   42

Education: Teaching Our Children

"Preparing our students for the future requires the support of teachers, parents, businesses, and the community. From participation in a mentoring or shadowing program, to becoming a partner with a local school, you can influence the quality of teaching and learning that takes place every day in Greenville County schools."

Chapter Four   50

Health Care: A Healthy Community

"Greenville's outstanding quality of life and its central location between the Northeast and the Deep South have attracted medical professionals who are the best in their fields. The Greenville area's tightly-networked medical system provides citizens with easily accessible treatment. Whether it is a routine treatment or a sudden emergency, Greenville's healthcare community is one of the most responsive and effective medical systems in the nation."

Chapter Five   58

Leadership: Governing the South's Crown Jewel

"In Greenville there is truly a unified effort among government, private interests, and the Chamber of Commerce to recruit and retain business in the local community. This cooperative spirit provides a synergy for economic development efforts."

Chapter Six   68

Athletics: The Sporting Life

"Weather you are a participant or spectator, Greenville's sport facilities and programs cater to your tastes. Professional, collegiate, youth, and pastime sports add a competitive dimension to Greenville that improves the quality of life for people who live and work here."

Chapter Seven   88

From the Art Museum to the Zoo: Greenville's Diverse Cultural Arts Scene

"The profusion of opportunities to see and participate in music, dance, theater, arts, education, and the visual arts sets Greenville apart from many other cities of similar size and gives Greenvillians an enviable quality of life. The arts have become a major component of how Greenville sees itself, and they are a continual source of pride."

Chapter Eight   100

Festivals and Special Events: A Season of Celebrations!

"One of the significant elements of Greenville's outstanding quality of life is the award-winning events that take place downtown. Spring and summer offer a busy event season with almost daily free entertainment for the whole family, while our fall and winter festivals are second to none. Our events make Greenville special."

Chapter Nine   114

People: The Cooperative Spirit of Greenville

"Greenville is a nurturing hometown…a place where people come together to address the community's needs, cooperate, and improve the quality of life for everyone."

Chapter Ten   122

Community: Sharing the Dream

"Greenville has a rich diversity of living environments for families relocating to the Upstate. No matter where you choose to live, you have convenient access to all the amenities that Greenville has to offer, including a thriving downtown, area parks, and remarkable facilities such as the Peace Center for the Performing Arts and the Bi Lo Center."

Foreword

A quality, culturally rich family environment; a winning spirit; and an ideal home for business. That's Greenville.

On behalf of the Greater Greenville Chamber of Commerce and its local businesses, we present this book to the Greenville community.

Within these beautiful pages, it is our sincere hope that you will experience the quality, texture, and healthy pulse of Greenville. We are rich in wonderful people, progressive partnerships, and exciting opportunities. As you enjoy this book, you will come to understand why our future is so bright.

With the approach of the new century, it's an exciting time in Greenville. Those of us who live here know and appreciate the warmth and friendliness of our people, respect our traditions and heritage, and look forward to many opportunities for a prosperous future.

We are proud to share with you a glimpse into the heart and soul of Greenville—a great place to live, work, and do business. But most of all, a place simply to enjoy.

Greater Greenville Chamber of Commerce

Prologue

By Max M. Heller

As you look at the Greenville of today, you will find a community as diverse as America. It is truly a mirror of our nation.

The spirit of Greenville and the leadership of the past as well as the present have made us what we are today.

And while we have enjoyed considerable growth over the years, we have always tried to preserve the "good" and kept in mind not to kill the goose that laid the golden egg. And so you will see beautiful land-scapes, the "green" in Greenville and all of the gifts of nature. As you see our beautiful neighborhoods, parks and our institutions of learning, healing, the arts, and recreation as well as public and private buildings, please know that all of these were made possible by partnership of the government and the private sector. It has been the history of Greenville for all people to work together regardless of their station in life. And much was created because of the generosity of private citizens and the business community.

The spirit of Greenville is such that we want to assure that everyone has an opportunity to succeed. More than 40 nationalities and people from all over the United States live here and we work together to make life better for all.

When I ask people "What brought you here?" The answer invariably is "opportunity" and then they say we came because of the quality of life here, we came because of the beauty of the land and the goodness of its people.

And when I ask people "What keeps you here?" The answer is the way of life, the people and the places, the economic opportunities, our neighbors, our friends, and our places of worship.

We are the recipients of unselfish dedicated leadership from all walks of life and we appreciate the contributions made by all.

So come and enjoy your visit to Greenville, and better yet, stay and become a Greenvillian. You are truly welcome here.

Part One

1

Chapter One

Greenville, South Carolina: Small Town Feel, Big City Amenities

Greenville's birthplace began near a beautiful waterfall along the banks of the Reedy River. Now more than 225 years later, that site has become the center of a thriving, prosperous international city.

15

After 5 p.m., the city streets come alive with the dinner rush. Visitors can select from a variety of restaurants specializing in nearly every kind of continental and international cuisine. Studio D Photographers.

M any have said that Greenville, South Carolina is a city with a small town feel and big city amenities. You can meander down Main Street, attend an open-air concert at the Piazza Bergamo, slip into antique shops and sip iced tea outside the distinctive bistro and encounter people you know. Greenville is a place where the future builds on the past, where tradition meets progress, and where cooperative spirit and cordiality rule. In Greenville, passersby on the streets say "hello," nod, and greet their neighbors with a smile.

The migration of residents from other parts of the United States and around the world has certainly created a cultural melting pot in contemporary Greenville, but the soul of this city is solidly Southern. From historic homes with white columns and spacious porches to the friendly greetings of clerks and bankers, the threads woven in Greenville's tapestry include Southern culture and economic vibrancy orchestrated by pioneering leaders both past and present.

Nestled at the foothills of the Blue Ridge Mountains in the northwest corner of South Carolina, Greenville is a star of the South. Located midway between

Opposite. **Greenville is a city on the move, experiencing phenomenal growth during the last decade and maturing as a center of international commerce. From its earliest days as a trading post settled by Richard Pearis to the expansion of the textile industry and diversification of the economy, Greenville has continually attracted businesses and families to enjoy the wealth of this community. While the changing economy has cast aside water-powered mills for computers, fax machines, and the latest manufacturing advances, the traditions of hard work, entrepreneurialism, and community togetherness still underpin this great city.** Studio D Photographers.

Opposite. **Main Street in downtown Greenville is an orchestra of sounds, sights, and energy that began to tune up in the 1960s as revitalization efforts gained momentum. Its wide sidewalks, old-fashioned street lamps, trees, and benches have earned the city a prestigious special achievement award from the International Downtown Association. Greenville also has been praised in the pages of *Southern Living* magazine.** Studio D Photographers.

There's something for every appetite at downtown restaurants specializing in nouveau, continental, Mexican, Thai, Japanese, German, and a world of other domestic and international cuisines. Studio D Photographers.

Charlotte and Atlanta on the Interstate 85 "Boom Belt," Greenville thrives with huge capital investments and hundreds of new jobs created each year as major companies select the city for headquarters and manufacturing operations. Today, the population of Greenville County exceeds 351,000, making it the most populous county in the state. Still, unemployment is at a record low, and the city is like a breath of fresh air, offering a pleasing climate with four seasons, pure water, and an enviable quality of life. Rich cultural and recreational opportunities abound in Greenville from the Broadway shows like *Les Miserables* and *Cats* at the Peace Center for the Performing Arts to professional sports and concerts at the 17,000-seat BI-LO Center.

Legacy of the Leaders

Considering Greenville's thriving economy and warm social environment, one may wonder who has continually tended Greenville's garden, allowing diversified businesses, cultural opportunities, and an energetic downtown to bloom. Visionary leaders with talent, foresight, and diligence have piloted this city into each successive era. They built roads, established the water system, and spread the word about Greenville to other places. Eventually, the outlying areas of Greenville proper blossomed with new subdivisions and shopping malls. As the energy shifted away from the downtown area, the rhythm of Main Street quieted. However, Greenville's leaders quelled this trend by attracting new construction and planning for the future—strategies that breathed new life into downtown.

Downtown revitalization began with the development of two buildings—the new home of the Greenville News-Piedmont Company in the southside and the "Daniel Building," a high-rise office complex in the north Main Street area. Once community leaders started investing in the downtown area, a caravan of businesses and other investors soon followed suit. The city's face changed as shade trees and spacious sidewalks appeared, creating an aesthetically pleasing environment and

serving as a catalyst for further development. While construction of the Hyatt Regency Hotel provided an anchor for the north Main Street area, the arrival of the Peace Center in 1990 fueled the revitalization of the city's west end, prompting the opening of the West End Market, a tri-level market complete with a farmer's market, retail stores, and office space.

Today, when you walk down Main Street, you will hear people talking about business and sharing personal stories about the straight or winding roads that brought them here. Families living in Greenville take pride in calling this city home because it is truly one of the most successful and well-rounded cities in the world; Greenville is a place where men and women of any race or creed can make their mark, buy a home, enjoy watching Little League games in the warm summer, and live the American dream side-by-side with neighbors who share a common work ethic, value structure, and desire to contribute to the next generation. ◘

The West End Market, a structure housing specialty shops, offices, and workshops for artists, is one of the anchors that brought new vitality to the downtown area. Urban renewal has played a key role in Greenville's mission to attract national and international business to the area. Studio D Photographers.

Spawned by new development, downtown revitalization changed the city's face as shade trees and spacious sidewalks appeared, creating an aesthetically pleasing environment and encouraging further development. Residents and visitors head to the downtown area to browse the numerous antique shops, galleries, and boutiques that have opened in recent years. Studio D Photographers.

By October, commuters leaving the city on Interstate 385 after a day's work can first detect crimson and russet patches of color on the maple trees. As each day and week passes, the scenic drive is transformed as beautiful colors, showing every palette of red, orange, and yellow, overcome the green trees lining the road. After a few days of Indian summer—when it's not uncommon to turn on your car's heat in the morning and air conditioning in the afternoon—fall takes hold and the leaves say goodbye to their branches...at least until next spring. Studio D Photographers.

When the cool winds of winter blow into Greenville, an occasional snowfall quiets the city by suspending most movement. However, the winter season is short-lived and Greenville really isn't the place for woolen sweaters or heavy coats. Cotton cardigans and a year-round jacket will do just fine. Studio D Photographers.

Spring, a season of new life and energy, is a favored time of the year among locals. Not too warm, not too cold—just a time to experience Greenville living during one of its most resplendent times. Some historians even say that Greenville takes its name from the area's lush greenery. When spring arrives, sometimes as early as March, the aroma of magnolias and peaches blend into one tantalizing fragrance. Daffodils and their colorful companions emerge from the earth, and in a seemingly overnight phenomenon, the dogwood and pear trees bloom. Studio D Photographers.

The Greenville spring blends into the sultry summer, sometimes quite early. As the mercury rises, children look forward to a summer full of adventures. Whether it's exploring nearby creeks and ponds or suiting up for a swim in a neighborhood pool or lake, Greenvillians are always up for a midsummer cool down. Reading on the porch, staying up past bedtime, and wearing shorts and sandals become the daily ritual. Many residents pack up for a ride to the South Carolina coast, spending just a few hours in the car before sinking their feet into the sand. Greenvillians easily cling to the summer culture, as warm temperatures persist. And, even though the school bells ring in the fall, it's not uncommon for Greenville children to cast aside homework for a quick swim in late August and September. Studio D Photographers.

   The twelve-story Poinsett Hotel was a focal point of Greenville's social life from the time it was built in 1925 until the 1970s, when it became a residence for older citizens. Known for its grand hospitality, the Poinsett Hotel replaced the old Mansion House that once stood in the same spot. The hotel is named for foreign diplomat and Greenvillian, Joel Poinsett, who is credited with bringing the colorful holiday flower called the poinsettia back to the United States from Mexico and thereby creating a new American tradition. Renovations to restore this historic building to its former grandeur are scheduled to be completed in late 1999. Studio D Photographers.

Downtown rejuvenation and successful efforts to attract major businesses have generated growth in the service industry. New hotels, restaurants, and malls are continually being developed to keep pace with Greenville's progress. Studio D Photographers.

The Reedy River in downtown Greenville is a symbol of the city's evolution from a small southern settlement to a dynamic modern city. When former Indian trader Richard Pearis settled the land along the Reedy River in the early 1770s, he could never have imagined that his Great Plains Plantation would become a major commercial center with all the benefits of a world class city. From the early days of settlement Pearis recognized that this area, once occupied by Cherokee Indians who rivaled the Catawba tribe and hunted elk, buffalo, had a bright future. Pearis established a trading post and grist mill alongside the clear, cascading Reedy River. Today, the Reedy River still courses through the city, only now the banks of the river are dotted with buildings such as the Peace Center for the Performing Arts and Bowater headquarters. Studio D Photographers.

26

Christ Episcopal Church was consecrated in 1853. The congregation dates back to 1820, when a group of lowcountry Episcopalians formed the St. James Mission. Studio D Photographers.

Just a short drive from the city, peach trees grace the landscape with branches outstretched to the sky. Many families hand-pick their own bushels for home-baked goodies or simply eat the fruit straight from the tree. Studio D Photographers.

No other single industry has influenced the city's economy the way the textile industry has, historians say. "Greenville's rushing rivers provided water power for several antebellum mills, but it was not until 1876 that the Camperdown Mill on the Reedy and the Piedmont Mill on the Saluda began large-scale textile production. At the turn of the century, a surge of building just outside city limits began to create a 'Textile Crescent' around Greenville's western edge," said Dr. Judith Bainbridge, Furman University professor and local historian. Today, the textile industry remains a vital part of the diverse economy, but the business community is also rich with banking, manufacturing, transportation, engineering, electronics, advertising, retail, merchandising, and other **services.** Studio D Photographers.

Opposite. **6,000 Greenvillians lace up their walking shoes each year to participate in WalkAmerica, the March of Dimes' annual walk-a-thon. Individuals representing companies join independent participants in April to walk the six-mile course beginning at Greenville Technical College, weaving through Cleveland Park, and covering several downtown streets.** Studio D Photographers.

2

Chapter Two

We're in Business

Greenville's economic vitality reflects the community's diligence to excel at the task at hand, pursue new business opportunities, and plan for the future. The city's geographic location, hospitable people, and solid infrastructure have allowed this community to achieve distinction, attracting businesses from all over the world.

Fueled by the never-ending expansion of the community, the county has more engineers per capita than any other county in the United States. With companies like Fluor Daniel (*left*), Rust Environmental, Lockheed Martin, and Amoco present in the Upstate, it's easy to see how quickly the numbers add up. Individual success stories abound in the Upstate.

Shortly after World War II, Greenville business leader Charles E. Daniel persuaded northern business leaders to build or relocate companies to Greenville. Guided by the motto "Builder of the South," Daniel, owner of Daniel Construction, personally visited Northeastern executives, explained the economic and social benefits of living in Greenville, and urged them to join the industrialization of the South. The fruits of his labors produced construction and jobs that benefited the entire state.

In 1983, the Fluor Corporation purchased Daniel Construction. Today the company, known as Fluor Daniel, plays a major role in construction both regionally and throughout the world. Studio D Photographers.

The textile industry has brought people and investments to Greenville, and many spin-off industries have formed in result. A cornucopia of small business owners with entrepreneurial drive and courage have succeeded in Greenville. In fact, *Entrepreneur* magazine ranked Greenville as one of the nation's 30 best cities for small business. From old-fashioned neighborhood stores to innovative advances in technology, the entrepreneurial spirit in Greenville permeates all facets of the small business community. Studio D Photographers.

*L*ocation! Location! Location! The familiar saying, "Location! Location! Location!" certainly rings true in Greenville. Located halfway between New York and Miami, Greenville is a midpoint on the East Coast, providing a fertile environment for businesses both large and small. Its ideal location is one reason the city continues to grow. From Greenville's prospering downtown to the outlying suburban areas, the community's economic success reads like a case study from a business development textbook. Greenville's economy has continually thrived with huge capital investments and record low unemployment year after year, even as other regions in the United States have weathered recessions and sharp economic downturns.

Positioned along Interstate 85 between Charlotte and Atlanta, Greenville is the buckle of the "Boom Belt." Many corporate

flags fly here—some from far away nations and others erected by home-grown entrepreneurs. Greenville's close proximity to the port of Charleston and to excellent local airports has contributed to its success, and its pleasing climate and quality of life attract families seeking better jobs and wholesome communities. Greenville's business environment, while once wed to the textile industry, is extremely diverse today with a multitude of manufacturing, banking, transportation, engineering, electronics, and service companies, all of which make the city churn with expansions, employment opportunities, and reinvestment into the community.

Greenville's business and social links to the international community have helped give rise to one of the nation's most outstanding airports. Recognized by the readers of *Conde Nast Traveler* magazine as the seventh most user-friendly airport in the

United States, the Greenville/ Spartanburg International Airport is another Greenville gem. The facility boasts an expansive terminal with fine dining facilities, a gift shop, an art gallery, and 13 departure gates.

Reflecting Greenville's cosmopolitan personality, the airport has added international transit capabilities by building a Federal Inspection station where travelers can clear customs with efficiency and speed. The airport has also added a cargo federal inspection station to meet the demands of local businesses. Eleven passenger airlines and three major air cargo carriers service the airport.

A Little Bit of Greenville Everywhere

To fully understand the prominence of Greenville's economy, simply look at the brand names of products manufactured here. The hard-working spirit and industry of Greenvillians touch nearly every

With coffee bars, brew pubs, eateries, and specialty shops, Greenville's downtown is a popular destination for residents of all ages. Studio D Photographers.

Leading international companies such as Michelin North America, Nippon Carbide, and Hitachi Electronic Devices have opened manufacturing facilities here—just a small representation of the more than 245 international firms from 18 nations present in the Upstate. Studio D Photographers.

New construction throughout downtown Greenville testifies to the city's thriving business community and its economic vitality. Studio D Photographers.

household in America. In the family medicine cabinet, one may find products such as Renu Contact solution, Arm & Hammer Dental Care Toothpaste, Scope, GNC Vitamins and Benadryl—all made right here in the Upstate.

In the kitchen pantry, hungry snackers can pick from Wise Potato Chips, PET Milk, Carolina Pride bacon and hot dogs, Peelers Milk, Piemonte foods and pizza crusts, Hidden Valley Ranch salad dressing and Sara Lee frozen bagels—even the Frigidaire refrigerator was made by Greenvillians.

Of course, we can't forget the garage, where local products such as Ryobi power tools, Maxfli Golf golf balls, and Dunlop tennis balls are stored, right beside the BMW Z3s and Perception kayaks, which are also manufactured in the Greenville area. ꆆ

Old textile mills are a reminder of the industry that put Greenville on the map. Throughout the downtown area there are reminders that Greenville's economic heritage is woven together with the textile industry. From the first Southern Textile Exposition held in 1915 in the Piedmont and Northern Railway warehouse to contemporary gatherings at the Palmetto Expo Center, textile industry leaders have flocked to Greenville to display their wares and learn about the latest manufacturing techniques, chemicals, fibers, fabrics, and finished goods.

To keep pace with the growing demand, Greenville leaders have continually expanded and upgraded Textile Hall's services, allowing the city to grow from the "Textile Center of the South" to the "Textile Center of the World." Studio D Photographers.

Greenvillians and residents from the surrounding regions visit the community for shopping, allowing the county to lead the state in retail sales and outpace coastal tourist areas.

Encompassing the regional two-story Haywood Mall, McAlister Square, the upscale Greenville Mall, and a host of strip centers on Augusta Road, Laurens Road, and other areas, Greenville's modern shopping districts feature big-name store marquees, while downtown Greenville has an eclectic mix of independent specialty stores featuring artwork, antiques, gifts, and apparel. Simply put, Greenville is a mecca for shopping. With 150 stores, the 2.2 million square-foot Haywood Mall is just one of the favorite shopping spots among local residents and other shoppers who make the pilgrimage from outlying areas to look for the latest in fashion, sporting goods, jewelry, and other items. Studio D Photographers.

On the line at BMW, workers combine their efforts to create the upscale automobiles. The workers and the community first celebrated the opening of the plant with a gala affair in 1994. The positive impact of this capital investment continues to ripple through the local economy as peripheral jobs are created and other companies such as Emitec, a German automotive parts maker, and Greenville Glass Industries, a Chinese glass manufacturer, select the Upstate for operations.

In addition to BMW, other international companies like Hoescht Diafoil and Michelin have selected the Upstate for their international operations. Studio D Photographers.

To view the quality craftsmanship of local workers, visitors may take a trip to BMW's "Zentrum" (German for "center"). Inside the semi-circular glass visitors center, you can catch a glimpse of the latest BMWs and peek into the world-class manufacturing plant through the eyes of a captivating, three-screen film shown in the Zentrum's theater. Studio D Photographers.

The Greater Greenville Chamber of Commerce supports existing businesses in the Greenville area and recruits new ones to the growing community. Studio D Photographers.

Greenville's business leaders keep a watchful eye on the pulse of the city's economy. Greenville's earliest leaders exhibited a commercial savvy that turned the area into the greatest textile-producing manufacturer in the world. The same commitment and knowledge, displayed by contemporary leaders, carried the city through economic diversification and urban renewal to make it one of the strongest international business communities in the United States. Studio D Photographers.

Greenville's culinary scene is ablaze with cuisine ranging from home-style Southern fare to exotic international dishes. Whether you're looking for an international delight or traditional Southern cooking, the range of restaurants in Greenville has just what you want. To satisfy the community's cosmopolitan tastes, an oasis of exciting restaurants has emerged along the Interstate 85 corridor. Many travelers stop to enjoy the Southern hospitality and fuel up with a full slab of ribs, a heaping plate of pasta, or a grilled chicken sandwich. Studio D Photographers.

The region's close proximity and easy access to the Atlantic Ocean, the Port of Charleston, and other coastal communities has attracted international companies that distribute their products across the globe. Studio D Photographers.

3

Chapter Three

Teaching Our Children

"Preparing our students for the future requires the support of teachers, parents, businesses, and the community. From participation in a mentoring or shadowing program to becoming a partner with a local school, you can influence the quality of teaching and learning that takes place every day in Greenville County schools."

— Dr. Rudolph G. Gordon, Superintendent, The School District of Greenville County.

Greenville County's group of exceptional teachers and dedicated staff, combined with its investment in the finest facilities, equipment, and learning material available, make learning a valuable and enduring experience for local children. For instance, behind the walls of the Fine Arts Center—the first public arts school in the state—students grasp watercolor brushes, practice the fine art of oratory, and perform perfect pirouettes. Students may enroll in classes devoted to music, dance, drama, art, film and video, metals, painting, photography, and creative writing. Studio D Photographers.

Furman University, known as one of the finest liberal arts colleges in the nation, is an independent co-educational institution located just a short drive from downtown Greenville.

"Furman has developed a national reputation in recent years for its efforts to promote experiential learning through undergraduate research and internships. By enabling students to combine theory with practice outside the classroom and off campus, the university is building a bridge between the 'ivory tower' and the 'real world,'" said Dr. David E. Shi, President of Furman University.

Today, Furman University's 750-acre campus features beautiful landscaping and a 30-acre lake that provides a favorite gathering point for students, alumni, and Greenvillians.

Founded in Edgefield in 1826 by South Carolina Baptists, Furman University was first located in downtown Greenville near the Reedy River before moving to its current site in the late 1950s. Studio D Photographers.

Gazing through the telescopes at The Roper Mountain Science Center, one of several extensions of the school district of Greenville County, you can peek at the stars of the galaxy and look beyond the boundaries of our world into unknown territory. The mesmerizing celestial phenomena remind us of the next generation of Greenville citizens, the stars of tomorrow.

From the wide-reaching public school system to smaller private schools, technical education, and campuses for higher learning, Greenville is nurturing the community's youth with knowledge and creativity that will ultimately better the community in which we live. The spirit of enthusiasm and the openness of young minds are met with the dedication of educators and groundswelling community support for education. The community breaks the boundaries between private business and education, fostering the development of educated, skilled citizens with innovative programs.

The School District of Greenville County, the largest school district in the state with a range of 800 square miles, guides itself by the motto, "Success. Nothing Less!" This spirit illustrates the continual drive of local teachers who share their lives with Greenville's students, revealing the wonder of reading, the excitement of chemistry, and the multiculturalism of foreign language. The district's growing body of 54 elementary schools, 16 middle schools, and 14 high schools has earned both regional and national commendations for excellence in education. Nine district schools have been named "National Blue Ribbon Schools" by the U.S. Department of Education, and the state has continually recognized schools in the district with the "Palmetto's Finest"

award, an honor reserved for the top schools in South Carolina. Outstanding facilities, innovative programs, and a focus on career development make the school district of Greenville County a model of excellence for all communities.

Parents who choose a private school for their children can select from a variety of quality, accredited schools in the Upstate. Christ Church Episcopal School, which offers a lower school, middle school, and upper school, serves more than 850 students on two campuses. Other private schools include Shannon Forest, located on Greenville's eastside, and Bob Jones Elementary, Junior High, and Academy, all on the 200-acre Bob Jones University Campus.

Bob Jones University, a fundamental non-denominational Christian liberal arts institution, enrolls more than 5,000 students from across the nation and over 40 foreign countries. The University, founded by evangelist Dr. Bob Jones Sr., has gained nationwide recognition for its religious-based curriculum and for its collection of sacred art, one of the largest, most respected collections of its kind in America. Studio D Photographers.

46

Educational creativity is prevalent throughout the Greenville County school district. "Magnet schools," representing a newer concept in education, offer students the added creative outlet or academic challenge they seek in addition to providing them with the solid foundation of a core curriculum. Students in kindergarten through 12th grade can attend designated "academies" in the "select schools" program to concentrate on communications, arts, science and technology, health, engineering, and other subjects. The district also offers Hollis Academy, a year-round elementary school. Studio D Photographers.

The Roman Catholic Diocese of Charleston sponsors Our Lady of the Rosary, St. Anthony's, and St. Mary's schools, and provides education starting with kindergarten. St. Joseph's High School, accredited by the South Carolina Independent Schools Association, offers a college preparatory curriculum at its downtown campus.

The Greenville area is also home to an impressive number of universities, colleges, and other institutions dedicated to the pursuit of higher learning. Furman University, an independent co-educational institution regarded as one of the finest liberal arts colleges in the nation, is located just a short drive away from downtown Greenville.

Likewise, Bob Jones University, a fundamental, non-denominational Christian university with one of the world's largest collections of sacred art, attracts students seeking a challenging liberal arts education.

Other four-year universities in or near Greenville include North Greenville College, Webster University, the University of South Carolina at Spartanburg, and Clemson University.

Greenville Technical College, the oldest and largest of South Carolina's 16-technical-college system, provides the training that qualifies students for jobs in health and nursing, business, computer sciences, mechanics, and other technologies.

Young minds are at work throughout Greenville County—sure symbols of Greenville's vested interest in nurturing the future's bright leaders.

The Greenville County library system operates several libraries throughout the county, including the main library on College Street in downtown Greenville, 10 branch libraries in surrounding areas, and the Law Library in the Greenville County Courthouse. Studio D Photographers.

Greenville parents invest time and care into local schools, as evidenced by the outstanding PTA membership found throughout the Greenville County school district. Such strong parent and teacher participation benefits all students in the form of activities and events such as the Augusta Circle Carnival, field trips, tutoring programs, and others. Studio D Photographers.

Through its innovative and successful educational institutions and methods, Greenville's school system demonstrates its awareness that today's children are tomorrow's leaders—an understanding that will help sustain the city's success well into the 21st century. Studio D Photographers.

As the lights dim in the Digistar Planetarium / Sciencesphere, the largest planetarium in the state, children and their parents recline and look toward the sky before they are transported into space to explore the mysteries of the universe. The science center's Charles E. Daniel observatory features a 23-inch refractor telescope—the eighth largest of its type in the nation.

The Roper Mountain Science Center illustrates what cooperation between public and private interests can accomplish. The campus includes five large buildings and outdoor education areas where students learn about life, earth, and a range of other physical sciences. Today, it is not only a gathering point for teachers and students, but it serves the entire community with recreational learning experiences. The living history farm, for example, is a favorite attraction at the Roper Mountain Science Center. Visitors step back in time to witness and experience what life in bygone eras was like. Studio D Photographers.

For technical education, Greenville Technical College—the oldest and largest of the 16 technical schools in the technical-college system in South Carolina—provides the training that will qualify students for jobs in the current economy. Greenville Tech offers associate degrees, university transfer programs, and certificates in health and nursing, business, and the technologies.

Greenville Technical College's three locations offer morning, afternoon, and evening classes, Weekend College, College on TV, and College Online.

Greenville Tech has been partnering with the business community since 1962, and this mission remains at the core of what the college does. "By providing custom-designed training and just-in-time education for companies both large and small, both new and long-standing, the college is key to making business and industry successful and ensures the continuation of economic and industrial development in the area," said Dr. Thomas E. Barton Jr., President of Greenville Tech. Studio D Photographers.

4

Chapter Four

A Healthy Community

51

"Greenville has become one of the most desir-able places in the nation to call home. The reasons for this are numerous, but are based on one core strength—a willingness and ability to encourage innovation without sacrificing tradition. Life in Greenville is characterized by a desire to maintain those qualities that protect and nurture the well-being of the community while broadening its hori-zons to include new opportunities."

— Frank D. Pinckney, President,
Greenville Hospital System

All residents of Greenville enjoy an extraordinary quality of life. Good health and healthy attitudes are reinforced by the city's outstand-ing medical community. Studio D Photographers.

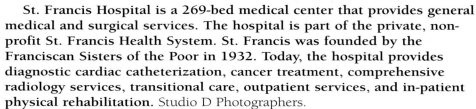

St. Francis Hospital is a 269-bed medical center that provides general medical and surgical services. The hospital is part of the private, non-profit St. Francis Health System. St. Francis was founded by the Franciscan Sisters of the Poor in 1932. Today, the hospital provides diagnostic cardiac catheterization, cancer treatment, comprehensive radiology services, transitional care, outpatient services, and in-patient physical rehabilitation. Studio D Photographers.

No matter where you live, keeping your family physically fit is a paramount concern. In Greenville, medical care is convenient, all-inclusive, and as personable and caring as a family friend. Greenville's medical community encompasses a depth of expertise, outstanding public and private facilities, and enduring dedication to innovation in research and care. As the regional hub for health care, Greenville's health system provides everything from prenatal care and routine infant immunizations to geriatric specialties and hospice care. Talented health professionals not only provide the most up-to-date treatment protocols, but also administer care with compassionate personal service.

Whether one needs a personal fitness program, diagnostic procedure, or complex surgery, Greenville's physicians, specialists, and nurses can take care of the community's full medical needs. Greenville has state-of-the-art private and public facilities that offer emergency, children and cardiac care, radiology, rehabilitation, and home health services, along with a variety of other specialized services. The local health care centers offer sophisticated diagnostic equipment including X-Ray, fluoroscopy, computerized tomography, scanning, mammography, breast imaging, nuclear medicine, ultrasound, and magnetic resonance imaging (MRI), as well as myriad other high-tech tools for diagnosis and treatment of medical conditions.

As the regional center for medical care in South Carolina's Upstate, Greenville contains eight hospitals. Five of the city's hospitals belong to the Greenville Hospital System. Greenville Memorial, the central facility, operates as the regional referral center with a level-one trauma center, a pediatric intensive care unit, and the region's only level-three neonatal

intensive care unit for the treatment of
critically ill newborns.

The private, non-profit St. Francis
Health System operates St. Francis
Hospital, including the Louis P. Batson, Jr.
Cancer Treatment Center, and the St.
Francis Women's and Family hospital on
the community's east side.

The Shriner's Hospital for Crippled
Children is the region's leading resource for
orthopedic care to children and teenagers. ◖

**Good health begins at birth. From neonatal and pediatric care to geri-
atric medicine, Greenville's hospitals work to improve and maintain
sound physical and emotional standards for all city residents.** Photo
courtesy of Greenville Hospital System.

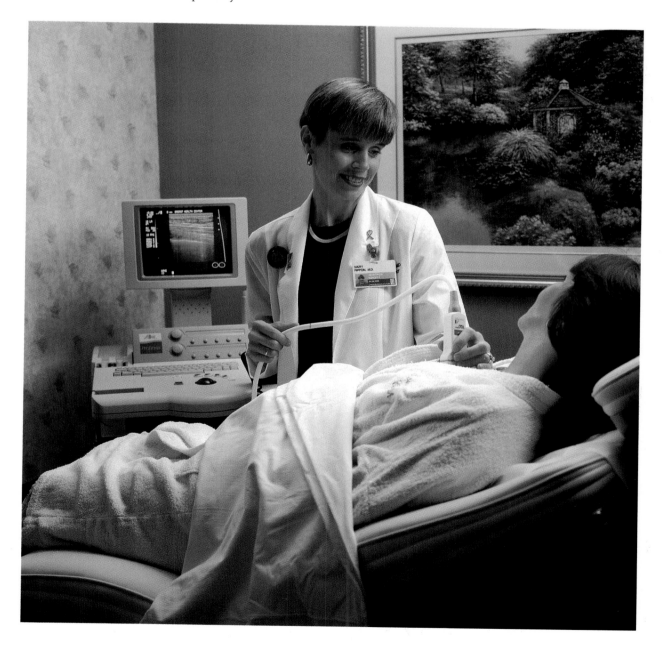

It has been said that an ounce of prevention is worth a pound of cure, and that familiar saying has certainly been embraced by the local health care providers that offer numerous health education and prevention programs in the community. Local residents can enjoy the health club environment of the Greenville Hospital System's LIFECENTER or participate in one of the many community education programs focusing on stress management, smoking cessation, prepared childbirth, and many other topics. St. Francis Health System offers the Vitality Center, a fitness and exercise facility including an indoor track, isotonic exercise equipment, and other fitness equipment on the grounds of the main hospital.

Jogging on the largest indoor track in the city, practicing the breast stroke in a 25-meter indoor pool, or performing circuit weight training are all activities individuals can enjoy at the LIFECENTER Health and Conditioning Club. As a center for recreational activities and health education, the LIFECENTER offers fitness programs, nutrition consultation, personal training, smoking cessation and a variety of other programs. Photo courtesy of Greenville Hospital System.

Whether you are suffering from a severe sports injury, heart attack, injury from an automobile accident, or other critical medical situation, emergency medical treatment is readily accessible in Greenville. Greenville Memorial Hospital operates a level-one trauma center and serves as the regional referral center for the area's most severe illnesses and injuries. Additionally, the St. Francis Women's and Family Hospital operates a 24-hour emergency room. Studio D Photographers.

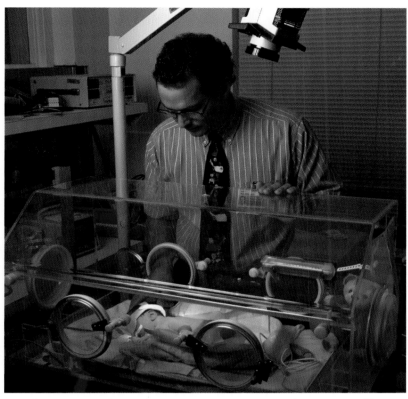

The Neonatology Intensive Care Unit at the Greenville Hospital System is a level-three facility that offers advanced care for critically ill infants. A skilled staff of nurses and neonatologists takes care of the infants until they are able to go home. Photo courtesy of Greenville Hospital System.

The drive to improve the quality of life for all residents manifests itself in ongoing research efforts that ultimately make a difference in the lives of individual residents. To bolster biomedical research efforts in the Upstate, Greenville Hospital System and Clemson University have signed an agreement networking physicians, engineers, biological scientists, and medical researchers. Together, the two institutions conduct more than 100 research programs pertaining to women's health, orthopaedics, surgery, pediatrics, oncology, and other fields.

By forging partnerships with academic institutions and leading national research organizations, Greenville's medical community is advancing knowledge about cancer and other diseases. The Louis P. Batson Jr. Cancer Care Center of the St. Francis Health System is affiliated with state and national research organizations, including the National Cancer Institute. The Greenville Hospital System's Cancer Treatment Center also conducts on-going cancer research. Photo courtesy of Greenville Hospital System.

The Greenville Hospital System operates Greenville Memorial Hospital, Allen Bennett Hospital in Greer, Hillcrest Hospital in Simpsonville, North Greenville Hospital in Travelers Rest, Roger C. Peace Rehabilitation Hospital in Greenville, and The Children's Hospital. Photo courtesy of Greenville Hospital System.

At St. Francis Hospital, patients benefit from the latest medical technologies and surgical procedures. Photo courtesy of St. Francis Health System.

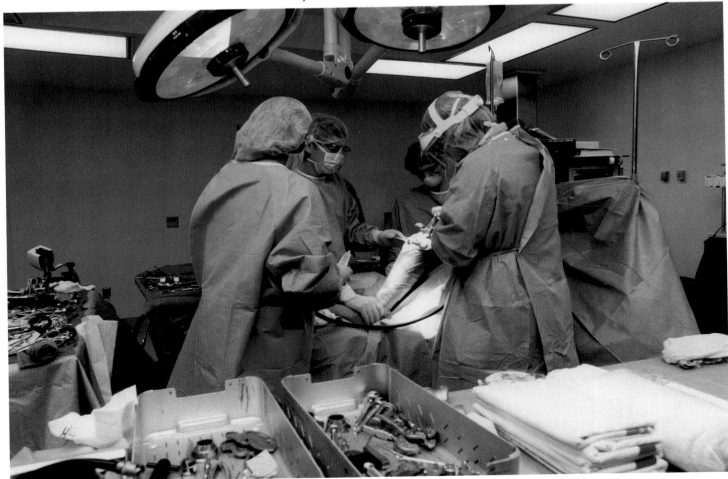

The Shriners Hospital for Crippled Children in Greenville is one of 19 Orthopaedic Shriners Hospitals in the nation, offering orthopaedic care for children under 18 years old. The hospital, which specializes in prosthetic fitting, scoliosis, spina bifida, and other orthopaedic problems, treats qualified patients free of charge. The Shriners Hospital also conducts extensive research into the clinical treatment of orthopaedic conditions and shares scientific findings with hospitals throughout the country. Studio D Photographers.

Greenville's exceptional healthcare system and medical community work to improve the quality of life for all residents. Studio D Photographers.

5

Chapter Five

Governing the South's Crown Jewel

In Greenville, there is truly a unified effort among government and private interests to recruit and retain business in the local community. This cooperative spirit provides a synergy for economic development efforts.

Greenville's law enforcement community stays in touch with local residents through community outreach programs. The Sheriff's Office and Police Department emphasize law enforcement strategies that allow officials to get involved in area activities and to advise neighborhood associations. Studio D Photographers.

Greenville's government officials have guided the city's growth through their leadership, legislation, and formation of public and private partnerships. Government leaders on state and local levels have diligently cared for the community's infrastructure, bolstering expansion in all areas of the county, especially the downtown area. Improving road maintenance, enacting better tax incentives, and spearheading business recruitment efforts are just some of the ways Greenville's leaders are working to enhance the city and attract new growth. Word of Greenville's business-friendly environment has soared beyond state and even national boundaries to capture the attention of several major international industries.

Public and private partnerships have spelled success for the economic development of downtown Greenville. Award-winning revitalization projects continue to benefit local commerce while enhancing the overall quality of life for residents. Under the visionary leadership of former Mayor Max Heller, the city of Greenville set out to breathe new life into the downtown landscape of the 1970s. With the input of San Francisco architect Lawrence Halprin, the city planted saplings, widened sidewalks, and strengthened the downtown infrastructure—revitalization efforts that improved Greenville's appearance and local color. Today, downtown Greenville is alive with outdoor dining, brew pubs, specialty shops, and special events.

City landmarks such as the Hyatt Hotel, the West End Market, the Heritage Green cultural arts complex, and the Peace Center for the Performing Arts are located in close proximity to the greenway system, a two-mile stretch of city park land in the downtown area. ◖

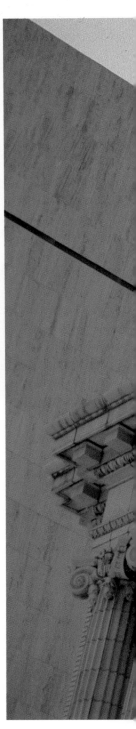

The Greenville County Courthouse features eight courtrooms. The judicial wing houses civil and criminal court, master of equity, and the court of common pleas. Private, secure, and public areas are separated to guarantee safety. Studio D Photographers.

Once housed in this historic building, the Greenville County Family Court handles cases involving domestic issues. Studio D Photographers.

Greenville City Hall, located on Main Street in Greenville, provides offices for the mayor, city council members, and other administrative offices. Studio D Photographers.

Greenvillians take responsibility for the future, sharing a sense of purpose—to make Greenville the most desirable place in South Carolina to work, live, and raise families. Studio D Photographers.

Greenville's law enforcement community makes sure that Greenville is truly a safe place to live. Community-oriented law enforcement gives local residents an honest feeling of security. The Greenville County Sheriff's Office covers the county with uniformed patrol officers. The Sheriff's Office is divided into Northern and Southern districts to minimize response times and allow deputies to get to know the communities they serve. The Greenville City Police Department controls crime in the city. Other municipal police departments operate in Travelers Rest, Mauldin, Simpsonville, Fountain Inn, and Greer. Studio D Photographers.

The Greenville County Sheriff's Office operates an OH-58C Kiowa helicopter to bolster local law enforcement efforts. The Sheriff's Office also has an Underwater Search and Recovery team trained to perform under crisis situations. By combining specially-skilled law enforcement officers with the most effective tools, officials can maintain a superior level of public safety. Studio D Photographers.

Despite rapid growth, Greenville County is still a safe place to live and raise a family. Studio D Photographers.

Illustrating government cooperation, the Greenville County Law Enforcement Center houses the Greenville County Sheriff's Office, The Greenville City Police Department, Crime Stoppers of Greenville, and other administrative law enforcement offices. Studio D Photographers.

6

Chapter Six

The Sporting Life

"The timing of the BI-LO Center project has been a perfect complement to the tremendous growth and development the Upstate has enjoyed over the last few years. ScheerSports is proud to be a partner in that growth and thrilled to be able to offer Upstate residents— both new and old—quality entertainment in a premier, state-of-the-art venue. There's no doubt the BI-LO Center will continue to provide many, many exciting new opportunities for individuals and businesses well into the next millennium."

—Carl Scheer, President of ScheerSports, Developer of the BI-LO Center.

Furman University's men's soccer team has dominated the NCAA Division I-AA league for the last 10 years. As important as winning may be, however, Furman coaches insist that education comes first. Furman student athletes boast one of the highest graduate rates among student athletes in the country, and Furman has produced more Southern Conference academic honor roll honorees than any other school in the league. Studio D Photographers.

Watching the dimpled golf ball curve along the beautifully manicured green of one of the area's noted golf courses before it gracefully plunges into the cup creates a great thrill—bar none, except for perhaps the excitement of watching the professional golfers during the Furman Pro Am, Thornblade Classic, or the NIKE Upstate Classic. Greenville's temperate climate gives golfers the opportunity to enjoy year-round golf on some of the best courses in the nation. *Golf Digest* **ranked The Cliffs at Glassy the fourth most beautiful course in the nation in 1996 and Chanticleer golf course among the top 100 courses nationwide in 1997.**

Greenville area golf courses, numbering 55 and growing, boast designs from P.B. Dye, Robert Trent Jones, George Cobb, Gary Player, Tom Jackson, and others. For non-golfers, the rolling green hills of the area golf courses provide a picturesque landscape, but for golfers of all ages and skill levels, the scenic greens provide a challenge. Studio D Photographers.

*T*he Greenville Braves baseball player swings the bat in perfect time, catapulting the ball into the sky. Children, cheeks bulging with bubble gum, rush to the edge of the box seats for the chance to catch the prize on its descent to the field at Greenville Municipal Stadium. The thrill of taking the game ball home is so close, it's almost within grasp. After all, this is the Greenville Braves, the AA team known for producing Atlanta Braves major league players such as Tom Glavine, Chipper Jones, Javier Lopez, Andruw Jones, and others.

Simply put, Greenville builds champions. It is the hometown to admired baseball player Shoeless Joe Jackson—the Chicago White Sox player who once played textile league baseball in Greenville—and it was the college town to LPGA Hall-of-Famer Betsy King, who sharpened her golfing skills at Furman University and who returns to the city each year for the Furman Pro Am.

Perhaps Greenville's outstanding record can be attributed to the fact that the city builds sports venues to support all types of athletes, from professional hockey players to four-year-old soccer players. Or maybe it is just because the passion for watching and participating in sports is a common emotion among Greenville residents.

Deciding where to go and what to do is the difficult part for sports enthusiasts. It's a veritable wrestling match between golf, football, soccer, fishing, bowling, and one of the many other sports practiced in Greenville. With the new BI-LO Center—a 16,000-seat indoor sporting venue that houses Greenville's own hockey team called The Greenville Grrrowl—collegiate stadiums, and phenomenal amateur venues including a year-round aquatic center, equestrian park, and ice skating rink, Greenvillians are always on their way to a sporting event. Professional and collegiate sports, plus a wealth of recreational sporting opportunities for adults and youth alike, contribute to the upbeat, competitive spirit that personifies Greenville and its people.

Recognizing that leisure, recreation, and the ethics of team sports contribute to the physical and emotional health of the community, local government agencies and private individuals have combined their efforts to support sports. The City of Greenville Parks and Recreation Department, the YMCA, and the YWCA have assumed key roles in organizing adult athletic leagues for sports such as football, softball, baseball, volleyball, and tennis. In a departure from mainstream sports, athletes are literally scaling the walls of the city's indoor climbing facility, designed to handle climbers of all skill levels. And, further breaking the convention of traditional sports, the city has rolled out an in-line hockey league.

The Greenville County Recreation District also contributes to leisure in the Upstate by operating 48 recreation sites on more than 1,000 acres throughout the county. Encompassing seven indoor facilities, 64 tennis courts, 39 athletic fields, seven picnic shelters, five swimming pools, and a number of other facilities, the Recreation Department is a vital player in improving the quality of life for Greenville's citizens.
Studio D Photographers.

The 16,000 seat BI-LO Center, located in the heart of Greenville's downtown (visible on the lower right corner of photo), is a multi-purpose sports and entertainment venue that provides area residents a variety of athletic events such as professional hockey, professional ice skating, NBA, and collegiate basketball, as well as family-oriented activities like the circus, ice shows, and concerts.

The $59 million center spans 298,000 square feet and is the largest arena in South Carolina. The BI-LO supermarket chain, headquartered in the Upstate, became the naming rights partner of the arena in 1995. It was the first time a supermarket chain placed its name on a sports and entertainment arena. The BI-LO Center has a lower bowl, upper bowl, and luxury seating. Studio D Photographers.

The latest addition to the professional sports scene is the Greenville Grrrowl, a professional hockey team, based in the BI-LO Center. The team thrills Greenvillians with daring moves on the ice and the unrelenting pursuit to win.

Collegiate sports are also an integral part of the Upstate sports scene. Where else would you find a sea of orange than at Clemson University's Death Valley during a home football game? Football fanaticism is rampant in the Upstate, especially during a rival game between University of South Carolina and Clemson University. The city galvanizes as alumni and friends of each school wear team colors, pack elaborate tailgate lunches, and watch the two teams battle it out on the gridiron.

The other side of Greenville's devotion to the sporting life can be experienced in the great outdoors. Since Greenville's temperate climate stretches the fall and spring seasons, hiking, hunting, fishing, camping, boating, and cycling are all ideal on the local terrain. Many residents take advantage of nearby Lake Hartwell, Lake Jocassee, and Lake Keowee, or retreat to the picturesque state parks nearby. Greenville residents seeking outdoor recreational experiences can find themselves hiking along scenic waterfalls after only a short drive from the city.

In Greenville, the healthy spirit of competition, the camaraderie of team sports, and the desire to push the outer limits of physical and mental strength underpin this city's athleticism. ◖

Ceremonies introducing the newly formed Greenville Grrrowl, the city's own professional hockey team, took place at the BI-LO Center downtown. Officials selected the Grrrowl nickname because it personifies the "never-say-never" attitude of the Upstate. Studio D Photographers.

The University of South Carolina versus Clemson games polarize Upstate alumni. Spectators don collegiate colors, broadcast their loyalties with flags and banners, pack tailgate picnics, and head to Columbia or Clemson's "Death Valley" for the game. The Clemson Tigers bring NCAA and ACC sports action to the Upstate with football, basketball, soccer, baseball, and other sports. Studio D Photographers.

Furman University boasts one of the finest athletic traditions anywhere, and it has invested significant resources in building quality athletic facilities, including Paladin Stadium, Minor Herndon Mickel Tennis Center, and the REK Center for Intercollegiate Golf. In addition to serving as home for the Paladin basketball team, the multi-purpose Timmons Arena hosts a score of other athletic events.

Whether it's football, basketball, baseball, tennis, or golf, Furman students, alumni, and family flock to the stands to cheer for their favorite team. Studio D Photographers.

Athletic programs are not limited to local schools and colleges. Community centers operated by the city of Greenville, the YMCA, and the YWCA help local athletes to take advantage of swimming pools, outdoor jogging tracks, ball fields, gymnasiums, and courts for basketball, racquetball, handball, squash, and tennis. The Greenville Department of Parks and Recreation oversees maintenance of the city's park system. At any time of the year, Greenville's parks are filled with activity, whether it's as quiet as a pair of rollerbladers or as lively as a music festival. Studio D Photographers.

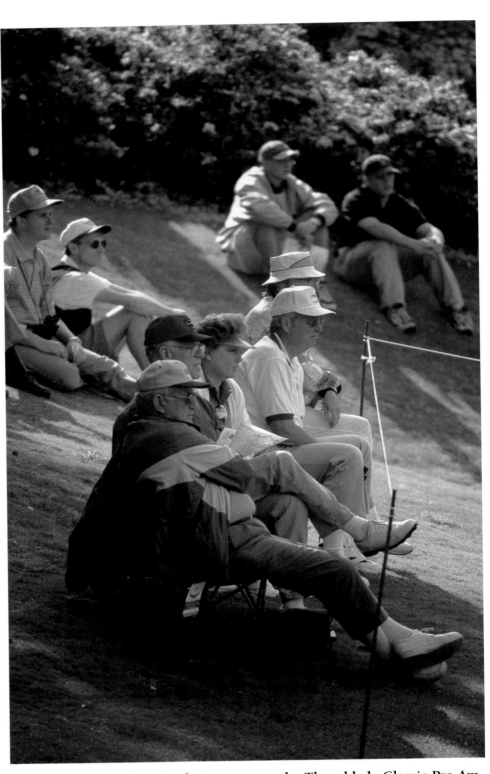

Recognized by the PGA for its success, the Thornblade Classic Pro-Am Golf Event, held annually each spring at the Thornblade Country Club, attracts world class golfers to raise money for local charities. Players such as Fred Couples (*opposite*), Jay Haas, Arnold Palmer, Greg Norman, Sam Snead, Phil Mickelson, Fuzzy Zoeller, Hal Sutton, Hale Erwin, and Davis Love have competed in past events. Studio D Photographers.

82

Sirrine Stadium on Cleveland Street is one of Greenville's most historic athletic facilities. Studio D Photographers.

Whether in a neighborhood pool or a nearby lake, many parents in the Greenville area encourage their children to swim at an early age. Widespread enthusiasm for competitive swimming has led to the formation of successful organizations such as the Swim Association Invitational League (SAIL), which includes hundreds of youth participants and is the east coast's largest membership amateur swimming association. Studio D Photographers.

The annual Furman LPGA Pro-Am, founded in 1982, has raised more than $1 million for the endowed golf scholarship program at Furman University. Furman alumni and LPGA Hall of Famers Betsy King and Beth Daniel began the tournament, which attracts fellow LPGA pros and amateur golfers alike. "I remember saying in college, when we were having trouble getting money for the women's sports program, that I would help those programs if I ever had the chance," said Betsy King. "Once I got on tour, I could see what a Pro-Am could do in terms of raising money." The Pro-Am has attracted professional stars over the years including Jan Stephenson, Pat Bradley, Nancy Lopez, JoAnne Carner, Kathy Whitworth, and Helen Alfredsson.

As the alma mater of such well-respected LPGA players, Furman University maintains a top-notch women's golf team. In fact, the Southern Conference has named Furman's women's athletic program the best in the league for several consecutive years, recognizing women in volleyball, soccer, cross-country, basketball, softball, tennis, and indoor and outdoor track and field. Studio D Photographers.

Soccer enthusiasts in Greenville also have a chance to see the pros in action. The South Carolina Shamrocks, a professional soccer team affiliated with the United Systems of Independent Soccer Leagues (USISL), challenge competitors at Shamrock Stadium in Greer. Studio D Photographers.

Upstate businessman Jerry Richardson scored big for the area when, in 1993, he earned the right to launch a new NFL franchise, the Carolina Panthers—a team the Carolinas proudly call their own. Greenvillians have taken loyalty for their new team to heart, dutifully donning the team's blue and black colors and displaying Panther pride throughout the year. The Panthers play at Ericsson Stadium in Charlotte, N.C. and practice at Wofford College in nearby Spartanburg. In 1996, the team reached the NFL playoffs and narrowly missed the chance to play in the Super Bowl. Studio D Photographers.

Photo courtesy of the Greenville Braves.

Affiliated with the Atlanta Braves, the AA Greenville Braves compete at Greenville Municipal Stadium. Well-recognized ball players such as Chipper Jones and Cy Young pitcher Tom Glavine played in Greenville before earning their big league credentials. Studio D Photographers.

Studio D Photographers.

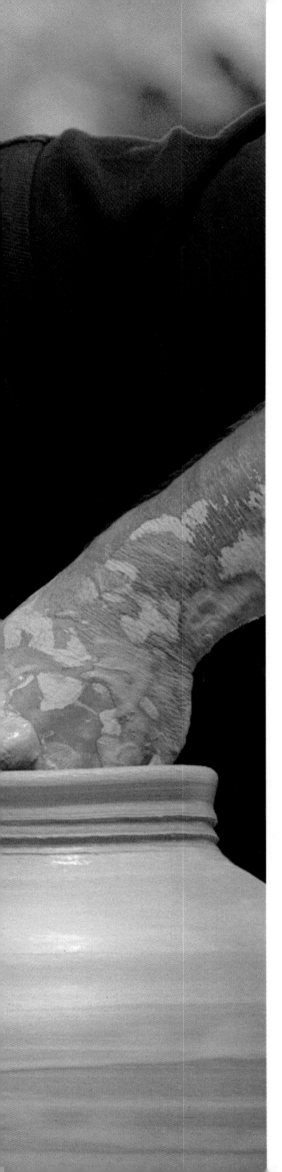

7

Chapter Seven

From the Art Museum to the Zoo: Our Diverse Cultural Arts Scene

"The profusion of opportunities to see and participate in music, dance, theater, arts, education, and the visual arts sets Greenville apart from many other cities of similar size and gives Greenvillians an enviable quality of life. The arts have become a major component of how Greenville sees itself, and they are a continual source of pride."

—Elizabeth Peace Stall, President, Peace Center Foundation (1985-1991)

The talents of local artists capture the attention of Greenville residents, whose steadfast patronage of the arts is evident in the city's myriad of museums, galleries, and special events. The city is home to many nationally recognized artists who have achieved impressive commendations for their works. Studio D Photographers.

The 400-seat Dorothy Gunter Theater provides an intimate entertainment environment for plays and concerts. Named for Dorothy Hipp Gunter, who donated $3 million in the original fundraising campaign for the arts center, the theater features catwalks on each side of the stage and a state-of-the-art stage floor. Studio D Photographers.

Famous architect Frank Lloyd Wright designed and built a home in Greenville's North Main Street area. The home is one of 19 homes nationwide that Wright signed by marking his initials in a red tile near the front door. The ranch style home, which spans 1,727 square feet, houses Wright-designed furniture. Studio D Photographers.

When The Peace Center for the Performing Arts opened in 1990, it literally set the stage for world class artists and entertainers to visit the Upstate, entertaining, enthralling, and enlightening area residents.

The cultural arts complex dominates the South Main Street district of the city and encompasses five facilities. The complex features the impressive 2,100-seat Peace Center Concert Hall, the more intimate 400-seat Dorothy Gunter Theater, the Coach Factory Building, which houses a cabaret and Founders' Room, the DowBrands Outdoor Amphitheater, and the Wyche Pavilion.

While Greenville's Peace Center complex provides a strong foundation for the city's arts, it is really an extension, or perhaps even a result of Greenville's long-standing cultural traditions. The Heritage Green arts complex, christened in the 1970s, provided the city's first cultural moorings: the Greenville Little Theater, the Greenville County Library, and the Greenville County Museum of Art. Both the Heritage Green arts complex and the Peace Center represent the value placed on the arts by the local community. Exceptional facilities and community patronage act as a magnet

for a range of professional theatrical and dance performances. Greenville is also home to a world-renowned religious art exhibit at Bob Jones University, an outstanding Southern Art Collection at the Greenville County Museum of Art, and the acclaimed Greenville Symphony Orchestra.

The South Carolina Governor's School for the Arts selected Greenville as the home for the school's year-round educational facility. The school offers students the finest art education available and brings renowned artists such as Maya Angelou, Tom Wolfe, Charlton Heston, and other guest artists to the Upstate. The School District of Greenville County's Fine Arts Center, the first public arts school in the state, is also a hub for amateur arts performances. The Greenville Cultural Exchange Center features significant artifacts of black history and the Emrys Foundation conducts poetry readings and publishes an annual book of local works.

The galleries of local artists capture the attention of downtown shoppers on the annual gallery tour and inspire budding artists who paint oil canvases, throw pottery, and practice fiber arts. The city is home to many nationally recognized artists who have achieved impressive commendations for their paintings and sculptures.

91

Greenville's thriving cultural arts environment beckons regional artists to the downtown area—a tide that has led to the establishment of unique art galleries and specialty shops throughout the downtown area. Residents and visitors alike enjoy browsing the galleries and shops in search of unique gift items, home decorations, jewelry, and other eclectic items. Studio D Photographers.

The art collection at Bob Jones University (*opposite*) is widely recognized as one of the most important collections of religious art in America. The Gallery of Sacred Art on the Bob Jones University campus contains 30 rooms displaying German, Dutch, Flemish, Italian, and Spanish paintings from the 13th through the 19th centuries. Visitors marvel at the works of Rubens, Rembrandt, Botticelli, Tintorello, Titian, and Cranach inside a spacious gallery that includes three authentic wood-paneled Gothic Chambers. The museum also contains the Bowen Bible Lands Collection, which includes an exhibition of 4,000-year-old Egyptian and Syrian scrolls and an 80-foot long Hebrew Torah scroll. Studio D Photographers.

Centre Stage-South Carolina! community theater and Warehouse Theater—South Carolina's only equity theater company—have built new stages and added performances in recent years.

Talented amateur musicians and singers perform in the Greenville Concert Band, the Heritage Chamber Society, or the 150-member audition-only Greenville Chorale. For local youth, opportunities abound: The Boy Choir of the Carolinas; the Carolina Youth Symphony, composed of middle and high school musicians who play a full symphonic repertoire; and the Greenville County Youth Orchestra, which performs "Young People's Concerts" in area schools.

Indeed, evidence of Greenville's artistic talent is everywhere, from the most elaborate professional touring shows to the amateur comedy showcase. In the park, in the mall, even in a gallery at the Greenville-Spartanburg International Airport—Greenville is alive with opportunities to observe, experience, and most of all, enjoy the arts. No matter what direction your muse moves you, in Greenville you will find exciting opportunities to enjoy the arts either as an armchair artisan or as a contributor to Greenville's rich canvas of cultural opportunities.

The Peace Center: A Community Achievement

Without the combined efforts of the city and the community, the expansion of the arts would not have been possible. Just as they joined together in the 1970s to revitalize the North Main Street area with the Heritage Green complex, city and community leaders combined efforts again in the mid-1980s to create a world class performing arts facility in the South Main Street area—one that would establish a focal point for the arts in Greenville, attract renowned artists to the area, and support continued development in the city's West end.

Under the leadership of former Mayor Bill Workman, the city purchased the land at the intersection of Broad and Main Streets and prepared it for construction of

Every year, the South Carolina Children's Theater hosts performances of childhood favorites such as *Winnie the Pooh* and *The Wizard of Oz*. Further demonstrating a commitment to enhancing art appreciation among youths, the theater offers instruction in drama and musical theater for area children. Studio D Photographers.

The Peace Center. At the same time, private fundraising initiatives achieved much success as the entire community became involved. Even the children of the School District of Greenville County pitched in 88 cents each to represent the 88 keys of a piano and collected enough money to purchase the Center's Steinway grand. This successful public-private partnership put Greenville on the map for touring Broadway shows and gave local artists a place to call home. ⌐

Programs at the Peace Center Concert Hall include a diverse mix of musicians, classical and pop stars, touring Broadway shows, jazz concerts, comedy acts, magic shows, and dance recitals. The Peace Center stagehouse rises 11 stories, allowing for dramatic stage sets. The Concert Hall features an adjustable acoustics system and a hydraulic orchestra pit that can be adapted for different types of performances. The Peace Center complex also encompasses the Coach Factory, the Shirley Roe Cabaret Theater, and the Founders' Room private dining room, which is located in the same building the Confederate Army used for manufacturing wagons for the Civil War. Studio D Photographers.

Downtown Alive, (*opposite*) an after-hours social event held each Thursday in downtown Greenville, is the Metropolitan Arts Council's major fund raiser. Since it began in 1973, MAC has served to initiate, foster, and support artists and arts organizations in the Upstate. With funding from business and industry, local and state governments, and foundations such as the South Carolina Arts Commission through the National Endowment for the Arts, MAC has been instrumental in the development of a thriving cultural community and a nationally acclaimed downtown area. MAC continually strives to increase funding for the arts. Studio D Photographers.

Local humor entertains guests at the downtown Cafe and Then Some dinner theater. Original scripts poke fun at local politics, economics, and social life. Studio D Photographers.

Centre Stage-South Carolina! is a professional non-profit theater that specializes in current play releases and classic performances of contemporary dramas, comedies, and musicals that have achieved critical acclaim. Studio D Photographers.

Located near the historic Reedy River, Greenville's Peace Center illustrates the joining together of history, community spirit, and progress, making a strong, colorful braid that reflects the diligence and determination of the community to support the arts. The Peace Center provides world class entertainment for local residents. It also hosts local performing groups, arts education, and outreach programs. Another significant purpose of the Peace Center is its devotion to imparting local children with an appreciation of the arts. Each year, more than 40,000 school children visit the Peace Center to see and hear performances for a nominal fee. Studio D Photographers.

The modern Greenville County Museum of Art is part of the Heritage Green Arts Center in downtown Greenville. Built in 1974, the museum features four floors of exhibition space, an art school, a gift shop, and a theater. Some of the museum's more distinguished exhibits include a renowned Southern Art Collection with at least one example from every major movement in American Art, and a growing collection of 20th-century American art with works by masters such as Georgia O'Keefe, Hans Hofmann, Andrew Wyeth, Andy Warhol, and Jasper Johns. The museum also hosts as many as 15 changing exhibitions each year.

The Museum School of Arts holds classes for adults in art history, design, drawing, painting, ceramics, photography, printmaking, sculpture, and other arts. Courses for graduate and undergraduate credit are offered at the museum through the University of South Carolina at Spartanburg. Studio D Photographers.

The 14-acre Greenville Zoo has won awards for its attractively landscaped grounds and is home to exotic animals from all over the world. Local residents have long loved Joy the elephant, who greets visitors. Animal enthusiasts can see the natural world in action as they watch a white tiger prowl, snakes slither in their habitats, monkeys swing from trees, and farm animals eat from the hands of young visitors. Studio D Photographers.

The Greenville Symphony Orchestra, which celebrated its 50th-anniversary season in 1997, performs in South Carolina and surrounding states. The symphony has brought acclaimed musicians such as violinist Isaac Stern to the community, and also performs with groups such as the Greenville Chorale (*pictured*) and the Kingston Trio. To support the Symphony, The Guild of the Greenville Symphony conducts an annual Tour of Homes, which opens the doors of model homes for sale to the public. Studio D Photographers.

Sponsored by Upstate Visual Arts, the Art in the Park exhibit takes art displays to an easily accessible, public environment. The non-profit group represents 300 local artists and conducts many exhibits, events, and workshops annually. Studio D Photographers.

8

Chapter Eight

A Season of Celebrations!

One of the significant elements of Greenville's outstanding quality of life are the award-winning events that take place downtown. Spring and summer offer a busy event season with almost daily free entertainment for the whole family, while fall and winter festivals here are second to none. These events make Greenville special.

The mass ascension of colorful balloons at Freedom Weekend Aloft is a spectacle to behold. 100 balloonists are invited to attend the event, which is held in the Upstate region each spring. The event has won many state and national commendations for excellence. More importantly, it provides Upstate residents with four fun-filled days of concerts, balloons, festival rides, clowns, mimes, storytellers, sports, and more. Studio D Photographers.

Without a doubt, there is a festival for everyone in Greenville—whatever your style, your interest, or your passion. The celebration of arts energizes residents and visitors each spring with the Coca-Cola RiverPlace Arts Festival near the site of the city's historic Reedy River. Fast becoming one of the region's most recognized arts festivals, the RiverPlace Festival has a juried art gallery and interactive arts activities for children, as well as spectator and participatory arts opportunities. Studio D Photographers.

With nationally recognized events that are strikingly creative, Greenville is a community of people who take the word "celebration" to heart. There is even a festival each spring to celebrate the community's Reedy River, a historic natural landmark that influenced the development of the city. There is never an excuse too small to get together and enjoy the fellowship of neighbors and friends, taste a new batch of Southern barbecue, and enjoy spectacular firework displays.

Celebrations of the arts, sports, and music create an incredibly busy calendar for Greenville residents. Organized events, parades, and hobby clubs allow people to share company with neighbors and thus fortify the community culture that makes Greenville a lively and fascinating place in which to live. Many events are open-air festivals, which take advantage of Greenville's spectacular climate. At the

annual Fall for Greenville food festival or one of the many arts festivals and community events, you may see a young couple holding hands for the first time, a parent cheerfully balancing a four-year-old child on his shoulders, or an older gentleman engaging in a sport that keeps him young at heart. No matter what your age or interest, there is a season of celebration for you in Greenville.

City officials say that permits are issued for events literally every day—sometimes two or three a day—challenging residents to take advantage of all this city has to offer. Nearly every night of the week, the sound of live music fills Greenville's streets. On Wednesday, Greenvillians can grab their blankets and stretch out to listen to music alfresco at the Peace Center's Dow Amphitheater. On Thursday, they loosen their neckties for the outdoor concert series, Downtown Alive, on the

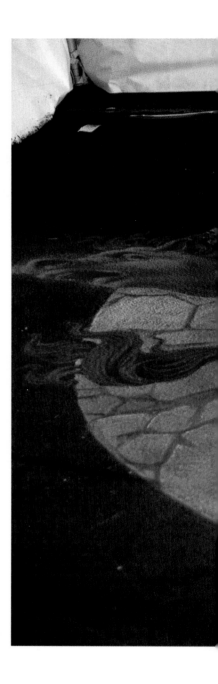

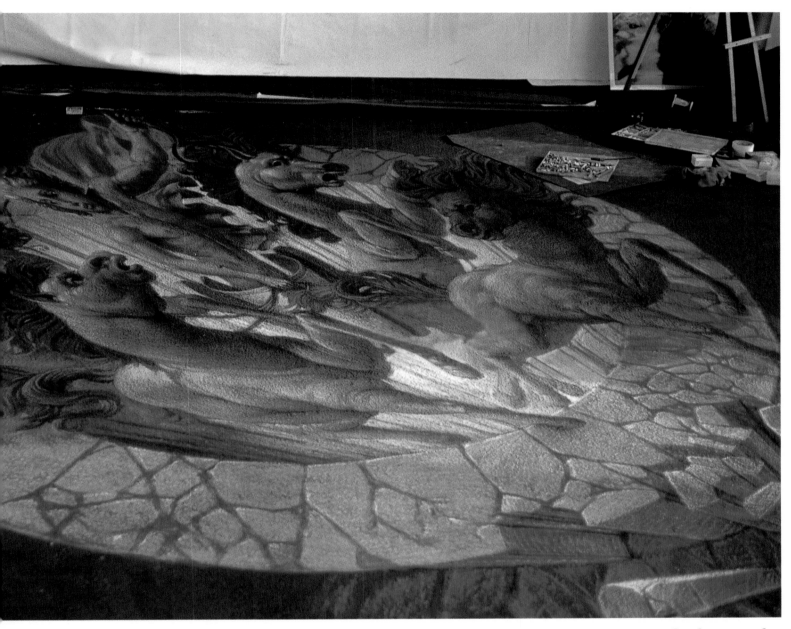

Recognized as one of the leading arts festivals in the Southeast, the RiverPlace Arts Festival culminates the annual Arts Week celebration in Greenville. The festival allows artists to participate in a juried art exhibition and gives local residents the opportunity to observe the arts, enjoy wine tasting, and pick their favorites from lemonade stands, funnel cake displays, and other food vending trailers. Situated along the city's historic Reedy River, the festival also celebrates the rich heritage of the community. Studio D Photographers.

Piazza Bergamo or maybe head to the West End Market to enjoy live music and conversation. Friday, the weekend is beginning, and what better way to unwind than at Main Street Jazz, held on the Hyatt Regency's outdoor plaza. On Saturday, it's time to lace up the dancing shoes for Shagging on Augusta, when dancers of all ages enjoy beach music and step in time to South Carolina's official state dance, the Shag, in one of the city's most prized neighborhood shopping districts.

Careful planning by organizations such as Greenville Events, the Parks and Recreation Department, and the Metropolitan Arts Council has allowed community events in Greenville to blossom into a healthy cornucopia of regionally and nationally recognized activities.

There is always a season—and a reason—to celebrate in Greenville. Whether it's simply the South Carolina sun or the arrival of a new season, Greenvillians take to the streets for festivals, making memories and creating community traditions that will be treasured for a lifetime. ✦

As the thermometer's mercury rises, activities for summer heat up. The Fourth of July explodes with enjoyment as neighbors and friends set up camp by stretching out quilts at Linky Stone Park downtown during the Red White and Blue Festival. With a nighttime parade, children's activity area, Red, White and 'Que Cook-Off, and a spectacular fireworks display, the holiday culminates in a burst of jubilation. Studio D Photographers.

108

Though the smells and sounds of summer may fade in the fall, the fun never subsides. Just as the leaves begin to change in Greenville, local restaurateurs pack up their wares and head downtown for the Fall For Greenville festival to serve up a profusion of food and fun. The aroma of hot peppers wafts from the Chili Cookoff and local chefs chisel fantastic carvings from giant ice blocks. The opportunity to taste the specialty dishes of local restaurants while watching street performers and enjoying live music on seven downtown stages attracts thousands of Greenvillians. Studio D Photographers.

World-class cyclists, including some who have competed in the Olympics, pedal around the city in the Michelin Cycling Classic during the annual Fall for Greenville festival. Studio D Photographers.

The heady notes of jazz float through the downtown air each Friday evening from Spring to Fall as part of Main Street Jazz. Greenvillians unwind at one of the downtown brew pubs and strike up conversations with friends and neighbors outside the downtown Hyatt Hotel. Studio D Photographers.

The virtual absence of extremely cold temperatures and snow in Greenville means that Greenvillians never have to say farewell to their beloved outdoor festivals. Greenville welcomes the new year with First Night Greenville, a celebration of arts and activities in the downtown area. The combined efforts of local businesses, churches, and city government sponsors over 50 performers from around the region in a dazzling array of special events. Every corner of the city comes alive with entertainment to please residents of all ages. Studio D Photographers.

Although its international community is constantly growing, Greenville hasn't forgotten its rich Southern heritage. Country festivals dot the calendar all year long, offering residents the chance to enjoy traditional Southern music, witness Civil War reenactments, and feast on spicy Southern barbecue. Studio D Photographers.

In recent years, Greenville has hosted the largest hot-air balloon festival east of the Mississippi, known as Freedom Weekend aloft. Studio D Photographers.

9

Chapter Nine

People: The Cooperative Spirit of Greenville

"Greenville is a nurturing hometown…
a place where people come together to
address the community's needs, cooperate,
and improve the quality of life for everyone."

—The Rev. Elizabeth Templeton,
United Ministries

Habitat for Humanity Greenville County combines volunteer labor, charitable donations, and raw building materials to create affordable homes for families who would not otherwise be able to purchase property. Qualifying families invest "sweat equity" into the home and agree to pay back an interest-free loan. Studio D Photographers.

The annual Greek Festival held at St. George Greek Orthodox Church in downtown Greenville draws residents from across the Upstate. The festival gives Greenvillians an opportunity to view authentic Greek dancers, browse the booths reminiscent of open air markets in Greece, and enjoy baklava and other Greek food delights. Studio D Photographers.

At the Habitat for Humanity homesite, a volunteer hoists a piece of lumber on his shoulder. Another volunteer hammers nails into the house's frame. As each hour passes, the structure is transformed from simple raw materials into a home. The foundation of a Habitat For Humanity homesite is a blank canvas where volunteers make their mark. With open hearts and caring hands, they build a family's house by doing whatever it takes to make it a cherished home.

A spirit of cooperation and generosity fills the air as volunteers in a city marked by tremendous success work to realize the dreams of a struggling family, to improve their quality of life. Activists with Habitat for Humanity Greenville County have built nearly 100 homes, including a 57-home subdivision in West Greenville called "Habitat's Village of Hope." Hope, generosity, and goodwill are values embraced by Greenvillians. Some say the kindhearted ethics of this community are born of the Southern hospitality that touches nearly every aspect of Greenville's social structure; others say such benevolence stems from the religious devotion of this community's people. While the origin of the community spirit can't be traced exactly, one thing is for certain—Greenville's giving spirit is both widespread and enduring.

Exemplifying the spirit of cooperation among diverse religions and religious denominations in Greenville, congregations from numerous places of worship come together to serve the Upstate's needs through United Ministries. The multi-denominational United Ministries reaches out to individuals and families in need, providing food and shelter and conducting numerous programs to help people acquire the skills they need to

The Greenville area sustains a diverse religious culture. While the Southern Baptist faith is predominant among Greenville residents, a diversity of religious groups including Education and Missionary Baptists, United Methodists, Presbyterians, Lutherans, Catholics, and many more worship at churches and synagogues in the Upstate. Through gymnasiums, swimming pools, organized sports, recreation, and outreach ministries, places of worship add a unifying dimension to this community and establish a foundation for giving. Many congregations extend a giving hand to the immediate community through Habitat for Humanity construction projects, food drives, and counseling initiatives. Pictured above is Trinity Lutheran Church on Main Street. Studio D Photographers.

find jobs. For example, the Life Skills program helps adult learners prepare for GED classes, while the Food Bank provides food to social service agencies and individuals in need.

Greenville's giving spirit is evident in its volunteer efforts and outpouring of financial support for creative programs that make a significant impact on the lives of individuals. At the center of local efforts is The United Way of Greenville County, which has organized charitable efforts in the Upstate for over 75 years. With financial support from countless local individuals and businesses, the United Way of Greenville County contributes to 45 health and human service agencies, which in turn assists 134,000 people each year, providing food, clothing, and other necessities. Greenville's dedication to philanthropy has

As businesspeople and their families have relocated to Greenville from other parts of the United States and the world, Greenville's ethnic and religious communities have diversified. Today, cultures representing many faiths are present in Greenville, including African Methodist Episcopal, Anglican, Baha'i, Buddhist, Christian Science, Episcopal, Greek Orthodox, Hindu, Islamic, Jewish, Lutheran, Nazarene, Quaker, Unitarian Universalist, Wesleyan, and many others. Studio D Photographers.

120

To raise money for charities that support children and the arts, the Thornblade Classic Pro Am Golf Event is held each Spring at the Thornblade Country Club. PGA Tour players including Jay Haas, Arnold Palmer, Greg Norman, Fred Couples, Sam Snead, Phil Mickelson, Fuzzy Zoeller, Hal Sutton, Hale Erwin, and Davis Love have played in the classic. Studio D Photographers.

allowed the United Way of Greenville County to achieve the highest per-capita giving in South Carolina.

People with unpredictable schedules don't have to miss out on the rewards of volunteering, thanks to groups such as Volunteer Greenville (a United Way service), and Hands-On-Greenville, (a volunteer clearinghouse for short-term volunteer assignments). Throughout Greenville, local volunteers serve food at the Project Host Soup Kitchen, deliver hot meals with Meals on Wheels, and hammer nails for the United Ministries' Adopt-A-House Program. Each year, Hands-on-Greenville conducts a volunteer-a-thon, once again reaching out to the community. With this overwhelming enthusiasm for volunteerism, Greenvillians have accomplished tremendous achievements.

The United Way of Greenville County supports the efforts of 45 health and human service agencies in Greenville, including the new Center for Developmental Services, a non-profit organization that focuses on evaluating and educating children with disabilities; the Golden Strip Human Resource Center, reaching out to residents living in the southern part of the county; and many other organizations that help families in need. Studio D Photographers.

While the community's physical needs are met by some organizations, the intellectual needs of the community are addressed by groups such as the Greenville Literary Association, in which trained volunteers share the wonder of reading with people living in the darkness of illiteracy. With enduring dedication, tutors train those who can't read in skills that allow them to read a book for the first time, fill out a job application, and write a letter. ▣

10

Chapter Ten

Community: People Sharing the Dream

Greenville has a rich diversity of living environments for families relocating to the Upstate. No matter where you choose to live, you have convenient access to all the amenities that Greenville has to offer, including a thriving downtown, area parks, and remarkable facilities such as the Peace Center for the Performing Arts and the BI-LO Center.

123

The scenic mountains of the Upstate represent just one of the many options possible for Greenville residents. The breathtaking beauty of Caesar's Head State Park and Paris Mountain State Park are two areas that make a more pastoral lifestyle possible for Greenville residents who prefer living closer to nature over the buzz of the city streets. Studio D Photographers.

Greenville's urban renaissance has led scores of residents to rediscover the excitement of life downtown. Cleaner, safer streets lined with shady trees and new glassy buildings reflecting images of the old, restored warehouses and mills nearby create the essence of Greenville's character. One result of these improvements is a repopulated downtown. Developers have converted many of the historic brick buildings into offices and apartments, attracting residents who prefer the special energy of city living. Many of Greenville's downtown apartments feature amenities such as hardwood floors and sandblasted brick walls—just footsteps away from the excitement of restaurants, galleries, and specialty shops. Studio D Photographers.

A sense of community embraces Greenvillians like a big hug. A drive through town reveals some of the community's simple splendors: azaleas blooming in the yards of historic residential districts, children playing kickball in the cul-de-sacs of suburban neighborhoods, neighbors working to landscape community entrances, and avid golfers swinging clubs on one of the area's many golf courses.

Despite the city's rapid growth and growing cosmopolitan flair, the grassroots values of a small community are still the backbone of Greenville. In the Upstate, lifelong friendships form, families grow up together, new neighbors settle in comfortably, and individuals achieve personal dreams.

Each region of the county offers a different style of living—the west side with its charming neighborhoods in Berea and Sans Souci; the burgeoning eastside area that stretches from the northeastern to the southeastern portion of the county; and the Golden Strip region. In the northwest portion of the county, families can purchase property in the historic city of Travelers Rest and enjoy unhindered views

of Paris Mountain. The proximity of the land to the mountains affords the opportunity for mountain living, without compromising the quality of life offered by the nearby city. Clean, cool lakes such as Lake Hartwell and Lake Keowee also dot the Upstate landscape, attracting residents who seek recreational, waterfront living.

For Greenvillians who prefer to live in the mix, the downtown area is a natural choice. In growing numbers, residents are moving into renovated apartments and condominiums above the busy downtown shops and galleries. The desire to walk to some of the city's hottest restaurants, enjoy a show at the Peace Center for the Performing Arts, or view spectacular window displays on the way home from work has set the ongoing trend in motion to populate downtown Greenville. And even though some people may choose to live downtown, they don't have to give up greenery; downtown Greenville operates many city parks that are linked by the greenway system, a two-mile stretch of public park. In downtown Greenville, yesterday meets today as newly constructed

The Reedy River Falls, which first attracted original settlers to the region, still provides a focal point for downtown activities. Today many shop owners and other townspeople who enjoy the excitement of the city center live in downtown apartments and condominiums. Close to the downtown area are residential districts containing some of the city's oldest homes. Traditional Southern architecture abounds in the historic districts, evidenced by homes with large white columns and red brick exteriors. The city has several neighborhoods designated as historic preservation districts, including the Earle Street, Park Avenue, Hampton-Pinckney, and Pettigru Street areas—all near downtown.
Studio D Photographers.

buildings stand alongside those that date to the city's early years.

Some of the oldest neighborhoods in the city extend to the North Main Street area, including the Hampton-Pinckney and Earle Street historic districts. Traditional Southern architecture, characterized by wide circular columns and breezy front porches, is visible throughout the older sections of town. Once in a while, singles searching for an apartment can snatch up a flat in the historic district—one that captures the romance of North Main Street's Southern architecture. The area is rich

with "fixer-uppers," giving families the opportunity to create their dream homes through renovations.

From South Main Street, Augusta Road leads to another charming residential area, known as the Augusta Road area. Just a stone's throw from the bustling shopping district surrounding historic Lewis Plaza, mature oak trees protect the large homes from the South Carolina sun. Narrow neighborhood roads wind around McDaniel Avenue, past the Greenville Country Club, and into well-established neighborhoods. In the spring, the crimson,

The suburban eastside reflects the bounty of Greenville's growth. With record-setting home starts and an explosion in the construction of retail shopping and dining establishments, the eastside attracts newcomers and longtime Upstate residents. With myriad houses, apartments, and condominiums available in a variety of price ranges, there's a residential address for everyone.

Teenagers residing in eastside homes attend some of the county's most prestigious high schools, and families have convenient access to golf courses, shopping centers, and recreational facilities. The eastside is also home to a number of executive apartment complexes and condominiums, giving residents an alternative to the traditional single-family home. Studio D Photographers.

The Cliffs at Glassy, located in the northern portion of the county, offers large executive homes and picturesque views of the valley. The Cliffs at Glassy golf course has achieved national recognition for its breathtaking vistas and landscaping. Studio D Photographers.

fuchsia, and pastel pink azalea blossoms decorate the stately homes, many of which have been in families for generations. Today, along Crescent Avenue—a prestigious Greenville address—large Southern-style homes are dutifully cared for by renovation architects and interior designers, while the grounds are tended to by landscape architects who preserve their mature trees, shrubbery, and flowers.

In the city's busy suburban eastside area, landscapers have a different challenge—planting greenery on what was once the Greenville countryside. Many families prefer a landscape dotted with pristine yards, cul-de-sacs, and neighborhood swimming pools. For them, the Greenville suburbs are the natural choice. In these new driveways, out-of-state license plates are soon replaced by South Carolina tags, once again illustrating the migration of residents to Greenville from other parts of the country. The opportunities for various lifestyles are virtually limitless in the Upstate. ◖

Throughout Greenville, families experience the everyday pleasures of suburban life. Children enjoy a round of kickball in the neighborhood cul-de-sac, play hide and seek among the suburban woods, or balance a bicycle for the first time, while adults share a conversation with a neighbor, plant a community garden, or take a leisurely stroll around the neighborhood. Studio D Photographers.

Several natural lakes in the Upstate region attract Greenvillians who either prefer lakeside living or just like to head to the lake for a day of adventure. Families enjoy boating, swimming, picnics, and other activities at nearby Lake Hartwell, located between Anderson and the South Carolina-Georgia state line. Lakefront homes accent the Hartwell perimeter, which also features private docks and a public marina. Lakefront living is also possible at Lake Jocassee between Pickens and Oconee counties and on Lake Keowee, east of Pickens. Studio D Photographers.

Greenville offers some of the most splendid golf course environments in the country, with courses designed by Ben Wright, Tom Fazio, and others. Near downtown Greenville, executives can move into a home overlooking the Chanticleer course of the Greenville Country Club, or settle on the eastside where the Thornblade Country Club offers new homes overlooking the private Thornblade course. North of Greenville, The Cliffs at Glassy and Cliffs Valley offer upscale executive homes in a golf course environment. The Cliffs at Glassy features one of the most aesthetically beautiful golf courses in the nation, with spectacular views from mountainous vistas. The northeast portion of the county also includes Pebble Creek Country Club, while Holly Tree Country Club and the Willow Creek Golf Course are found in the Southern region. Studio D Photographers.

While they work hard, Greenvillians play hard, too. Greenville's parks provide a respite from busy day-to-day activities. Families can enjoy a swing and a game or two at Cleveland Park, visit the Reedy River Falls Historic Park, or take a journey along the Timmons Park Mountain Bike Trail. Studio D Photographers.

Epilogue

By Dr. Judith T. Bainbridge
Director of Educational Services and
Associate Professor of English, Furman University

Welcome signs have greeted new Greenvillians since 1770, when Irishman Richard Pearis set up his trading post and grist mill on the Reedy River. North Carolinian Vardry McBee began village development in 1815. Pickens native Benjamin Perry studied at the Male Academy in 1822 and remained to become Reconstruction governor in 1865. Thomas Gower came from Maine in 1838 to apprentice at the Coach factory, and he remained a force in the community for the next fifty years. At the turn of the century, Thomas Parker arrived from Philadelphia to run Monaghan Mill; he would start our library, establish Phillis Wheatley Center, and help create the Parker School District. Charlie Daniel brought his construction company from Anderson; Max Heller his community commitment from Austria.

And why not? The boomtown of the 1990s evolved from a 19th-century health resort to an "educational Athens" (complete with two colleges and a seminary), from the "Textile Center of the South" to a bustling metropolis because of its geography—its narrow rushing rivers, moderate climate, glorious mountain views—and because of its people. From trading post to courthouse town, from sleepy Southern city to increasingly cosmopolitan center with expanding suburbs and international investment, Greenville has been blessed both by nature and with the foresight to absorb new ideas and welcome new residents.

"There is more gold than grace in Greenville," Bishop Francis Asbury commented in 1805. There certainly has been gold. In the past, profits from textile mills, from agriculture, retailing, and transportation; now from tires, automobiles, construction, health and education. But there is, and has been, grace as well. If Greenville, in the often-repeated cliché, is the "buckle on the Bible Belt," replete with hundreds of churches, it is also a county which integrated its schools "with grace and style." And grace of another sort continues today: Main Street strollers recognize it; the airport's frequent fliers feel it; visitors acknowledge its leisurely pace and gentle manners. Children—many of them—still say "sir" and "ma'am;" adults stop to give directions; newcomers are invited to participate in community life.

And for the future? Greenville is changing, as it has always changed. New neighbors will join the old; new industries will bring more jobs; streets and highways will become more congested; suburbs will expand. That much we can predict. Yet if history holds true, as so often it does, we will welcome the growth with grace. Those who come will stay.

Welcome.

Part Two

11

Chapter Eleven

Building
Greater Greenville

Coldwell Banker Caine
Real Estate

C aine Realty and Mortgage, then Caine Company, and now Coldwell Banker Caine Real Estate, has established a rich heritage in the 65 years serving Greenville and the Upstate of South Carolina.

Times have changed, but the company's reputation and focus remain "service beyond the contract," offering quality real estate services to customers and clients.

The latest venture, affiliating with Coldwell Banker, the number one name in real estate, enhances the ongoing commitment to professionalism. Caine is a full service commercial, residential, and relocation company founded in 1933 by Robert M. "Bubber" Caine, a man of great vision. With Caine's full time, experienced, real estate professionals, and the trust gained from business associates and friends throughout the years, Caine's reputation has grown, as have the size and scope of the company. Caine's prominence in the Upstate real estate market was enhanced by the 1994 purchase of Grier & Company in Spartanburg and the 1997 purchase of Coldwell Banker Newton's two offices in Spartanburg and Coldwell Banker Century Associates' two offices in Greenville. By joining together the Caine

Caine Realty & Mortgage—1933.

resources with these well-established firms, a locally owned firm was created with regional and national resources providing qualified sales associates throughout the Upstate of South Carolina.

As a third-generation, family-owned and operated business, Caine has beaten the odds by continuing to thrive from generation to generation. After joining the firm in 1953, Frank Halter has been president of the company since 1968. Under his direction, Caine Company has grown from 6 associates to 150 great people doing extraordinary things, which continues the tradition of superior real estate services.

Today, Brad Halter, a grandson of R. M. Caine, serves as a vice president and broker-in-charge of the company with direct responsibility for the residential brokerage operation. Another grandson, Caine Halter, a vice president, manages the commercial brokerage division and recently served as the President of the Greater Greenville Association of Realtors. They are both past Presidents of the Greater Greenville Association of Realtors Multiple Listing Service and have served as association directors and numerous committee chairs.

Caine's Residential Group consistently

R.M. "Bubber" Caine on Main Street in the late 1940s.

demonstrates outstanding production and professionalism, making it the premier residential brokerage office in the Upstate of South Carolina in terms of market share and total dollar volume sold. The company's residential sales associates boast the highest production per sales associate, and therefore per office, of all of the other firms in the Greater Greenville Association of Realtors. They have enjoyed this position over many years because of their attention to detail and by focusing on client needs. The average experience level per Caine residential sales associate is more than 15 years in the Greenville and Spartanburg markets respectively. All of the sales associates have earned advanced sales designations from the National Association of Realtors. Their sales associates truly understand the business of residential real estate, and know that continuing education is critical in order to remain on the leading edge of the industry.

Coldwell Banker Caine also has an active relocation department, which is a market leader in working with transferring

employees to Greenville's large corporate community. Caine's affiliation with Coldwell Banker and their network of over 62,000 sales associates and 2,700 offices offers quality relocation services to or from any location. Coldwell Banker Caine also keeps a close eye locally for new business development and business expansion opportunities. They are consistently calling on and servicing more than 200 corporations such as Michelin, BMW, Lockheed, Sterling Diagnostic Imaging, Hitachi, Cryovac, and the Greenville Hospital System. For the past ten years, Caine has been involved with almost every major corporate headquarters' relocation and assists hundreds of transferees each year. Caine's relocation group knows how to provide the information necessary for a smooth and pleasurable move.

The residential property management department markets quality homes for lease and offers the homeowner professional management in order to maximize the value of their leased properties. This department also gives the buyer clients and customers an alternative to purchasing a home.

(left to right) Brad Halter, Frank Halter, and Caine Halter celebrating Frank's 40 years with the company.

The Commercial Department at Coldwell Banker Caine consistently maintains a very high market share of the commercial business in the Upstate and their commercial associates average 12 years experience in the market. Five associates have obtained the prestigious CCIM (Certified Commercial Investment Member) designation, more than any other company in the state—an indication of Caine's commitment to professionalism and education. Coldwell Banker Caine can offer national and international reach through its commercial membership in Coldwell Banker Commercial, founded in 1910.

Their commercial specialists provide professional services ranging from site acquisition and disposition, landlord and tenant representation, leasing, property and asset management, and development. In addition to brokerage services, Coldwell Banker Caine Commercial also provides management expertise to our clients. Currently, in excess of 1.5 million square feet of commercial, office, warehouse, and retail space is managed within the portfolio. To ensure customers receive the treatment and service they expect, Coldwell Banker Caine enlists only the best and most qualified people available in the market.

"We're extremely focused on the impact technology is having on the real estate industry," Brad Halter says. "We make it a goal to stay ahead of the competition and offer our customers the most up-to-date services available anywhere."

Maintaining its own website on the Internet, www.cainerealestate.com, Caine posts its services and listings as well as general information on Greenville and Spartanburg. Not only does this alert interested buyers to available property, it also informs them of the area, promoting it for relocation.

After more than six decades of continuous operations in Greenville and the Upstate, the sales associates and staff of Coldwell Banker Caine work diligently to give back to the community by strongly supporting the United Way, building a home with Habitat For Humanity, or volunteering time to the numerous worthwhile civic and charitable organizations throughout the community. Their efforts have made them the number one commercial and residential real estate group in the Upstate of South Carolina. Coldwell Banker Caine continues to prosper and grow, always with an eye toward superior service in the future. ◙

The Harper Corporation-General Contractors

As it approaches its 50th anniversary, the Harper Corporation-General Contractors can celebrate a proud history of playing an integral role in what Greenville and the Upstate of South Carolina have become.

Integrity has been the philosophical cornerstone of the Harper Corporation, since John Harper, Sr. and his son, John Harper, Jr. founded the firm in 1950 in the back of a hardware store. Doug Harper, current president, and his brother John Harper III, corporate secretary, represent the third generation of the Harper family intent on maintaining the firm's extraordinary leadership role in the local construction market.

The reputation of the Harper Corporation is second to none in the area and has resulted in continuing business relationships with many of the leading companies in and around Greenville. Among the guiding principles of the firm is: "Being selective in choosing our clients and seeking long-term relationships through

Gathered in the elegant lobby of the Ogletree Building in downtown Greenville, the management team of the Harper Corporation includes, left to right, David Wise, John Harper III, John Harper, Jr., Doug Harper, Rick Richardson, and Ed Taylor.

partnering and total customer satisfaction." Harper Corporation's record lends ample evidence that this is a goal the company continues to achieve.

A shining example of the success of such a partnering approach has been the relationship between Harper Corporation and BI-LO. Proving itself one store at a time, Harper Corporation has now constructed more than 150 BI-LO supermarkets. BI-LO is just one of the many companies that put their trust and confidence in a company firmly grounded around a commitment to provide quality, on-time construction, professional service, and outstanding value.

"We pride ourselves on being a focused and financially strong company," said Doug Harper. "My grandfather and father gave this company a solid foundation, and under their leadership, the company prospered and built its reputation. Today, we remain dedicated to being the kind of general contractor that excellent companies want to do business with. We are very much a Greenville company. I can't imagine being anywhere else. We're proud of the role the company has been able to play in the progress of this dynamic area."

The development of the Harper Corporation into one of the premier construction companies in the area has been built around an extremely high level of customer satisfaction. The result is that many local companies simply won't use anyone else.

Working in the commercial, industrial, and institutional markets, Harper Corporation has become especially noted for its commercial work. Harper Corporation consistently ranks among the top 50 contractors in the nation in terms of retail construction, according to national publications.

One of the most prestigious business addresses in Greenville is the new Piedmont SouthTrust Building in downtown Greenville, built by the Harper Corporation.

The client list of the Harper Corporation reads like a Who's Who of Business in the Upstate. A partial list of clients includes BI-LO, Winn-Dixie, Publix, Harris-Teeter, Food Lion, Greenville Hospital System, St. Francis Hospital, CVS/pharmacy, Eckerd, Park Place Corporation, Mt. Vernon Mills, Grand Home Furnishings, Smith Dray Lines, TJ Maxx, Poinsett Hotel, First Union National Bank, Jervey Eye Clinic, Orders Distributing, Greenville Tech, the Peace Center, the Ogletree Law Firm, the Wyche Law Firm, and the American Red Cross. Harper has ongoing relationships with the key developers, architects, and engineers in the Upstate.

"There are several qualities which set Harper Corporation apart," detailed Doug Harper. "Foremost is our core of dedicated, loyal employees and our commitment to them. Not only are my brother John and I the third generation of our family in this company, but we also have many employees who share that distinction within their own families. We set a high priority on providing full work weeks, opportunity for advancement, training, a safe workplace, and fair compensation. Among our superintendents, we employ more graduates of the prestigious Project SuperVision program of the Carolinas

AGC than any other company in the industry.

"Secondly, we are extremely client oriented," continued Harper. "We work to develop long-term relationships, and we have a large number of loyal repeat customers. More than 75 percent of our work is negotiated. We provide a high level of service to our clients, including conceptual budgeting, value engineering, constructability analysis, and risk assessment."

"Finally, we have a strong commitment to give back to this community. This is evidenced by our broad base of community service projects and our support of charities, schools, and the arts."

A Harper Corporation design-build project, the new headquarters for Smith Dray Lines is strategically located just off Interstate 85.

"Harper was part of our project team from the very beginning," said Jimmy Orders, president of Park Place Corporation. The facility, with 20,000 square feet of offices and a 130,000 square foot mattress manufacturing plant, is located just south of Greenville on Highway 25.

Harper Corporation has been recognized for excellence on many occasions. The company has consistently earned the Award of Excellence for Safety Performance from the Carolinas AGC. Its Huguenot Mill Renovation was recognized as First Runner-Up for the AGC Pinnacle Achievement Award as 1995 Construction Project of the Year. The Ogletree Building on Main Street in Greenville was a Pinnacle Award Semi-Finalist as 1993 Construction Project of the Year. Harper Corporation is listed among South Carolina's Top 100 Firms by Arthur Andersen & Co.

The work of the Harper Corporation has gone beyond the ordinary on many occasions. In 1995, Harper was selected to construct an 80-foot steel and wood suspension bridge in a rugged and remote wilderness area overlooking Raven Cliff Falls in Caesar's Head State Park.

Raven Cliff Falls is the second tallest waterfall in the Southeast. The bridge was the brainchild of Greenville lawyer and naturalist Tommy Wyche, who thought a bridge over the falls would provide hikers with a birds-eye view of the spectacular falls.

Harper Corporation was selected to tackle the challenge. The materials were hauled into the remote site by trail volunteers. The project took six months to complete and was particularly enjoyed by the Harper workers involved. On their

The new "Concept Store" on North Pleasantburg Drive is one of more than 150 stores the Harper Corporation has built for BI- LO.

daily hikes to and from the job site, they frequently encountered the wildlife of the area, including deer, bear, and wild turkey.

Harper Corporation has purchased the historic Carolina Supply Building in downtown Greenville, with plans to renovate the building into a new company office and additional lease space. The building was designed by J.E. Sirrine himself and was completed in 1914. It will be carefully renovated to preserve the history, character, and charm of the old structure. The Harper Corporation has stepped forward to preserve this historic building, which was at one time scheduled for demolition. The building is now listed on the National Register of Historic Places.

Harper's investment in its new headquarters downtown is another example of a local company demonstrating its commitment to the community.

While the Harper Corporation looks back with pride on its 50 years of accomplishments in the Upstate construction market, its focus is clearly on the future and the accomplishments that lie ahead. The Harper Corporation will continue to pursue its mission to be "one of the premier construction organizations, dedicated to high standards of quality, professionalism, and ethical practice."

Prudential C. Dan Joyner Realtors

For nearly 35 years, Prudential C. Dan Joyner Realtors has enjoyed success beyond the founder and president's best expectations.

C. Dan Joyner, who was born and raised in Greenville, graduated from Furman University in 1959 as president of his class. After returning to Greenville in 1962 from the U.S. Army Intelligence Corps, he found the local job market difficult. In 1964, Joyner became Greenville's leading real estate agent with a successful local real estate company. However, Joyner had a vision to begin his own company, and so, that same year he ventured into the marketplace as a young entrepreneur with a dream of succeeding, and succeed he has.

Joyner has always held deep personal convictions about his hometown. He says he always finds himself promoting the high quality of life and the endless number of amenities the city boasts, including

Prudential C. Dan Joyner Realtors oversees eleven branches and over 200 employees throughout the Greenville/Spartanburg area.

the new BI-LO Center, the Peace Center for the Performing Arts, and much more.

"We enjoy such a high-quality of living here, including a low-crime rate, mild climate, and proximity to so many things to do. I think we sometimes take for granted the wonderful location we live in," Joyner says.

When Joyner opened the doors to his initial operation, it was a small cramped office with just enough room for himself and a single agent. Today, Prudential C. Dan Joyner Realtors is headquartered on North Pleasantburg Drive and oversees eleven branches and over 200 employees throughout the Greenville/Spartanburg area alone.

Joyner says his company has been blessed with good, hard-working people with high ethical standards, who enjoy helping others obtain home ownership. These same people have made Prudential C. Dan Joyner Realtors what it is today.

"We have never had a lot of turnover in our offices, and that can be attributed to our effort to make our employees feel part of a close-knit family," Joyner says. "We strongly emphasize training and we believe to run a successful business, you must help your agents define a career path in order to make them successful as individuals."

The Prudential name is recognized by 98 percent of all Americans. This is attributed to the fact that Prudential has an outstanding national reputation—6 out of every 10 Americans conduct business with a Prudential company. Prudential's local affiliations networked with their outstanding national presence provides customers with many advantages.

C. Dan Joyner, founder of Prudential C. Dan Joyner Realtors

Their "The Power to Perform" marketing campaign is built on the principles of strength, trust, and commitment.

Prudential also maintains a strong Internet presence throughout the world offering on-line services such as their National Relocation Service, which provides anyone in the United States the ability to enter a Prudential office and find the availability of the market anywhere else in the country. People looking to relocate to the Greenville/Spartanburg area can easily access the local market from any of the 1,400 offices nationally via the Internet. Such services and up-to-date technology position Prudential as the leading realty company in the Upstate.

Knowledge of the local community, Joyner says, is what keeps Prudential C. Dan Joyner Realtors at the top of the residential real estate market. This knowledge also carries over into the leadership roles Joyner and the company have taken in civic affairs as well.

"We have a responsibility to give back to our community," says Joyner. "We love for our people to be involved in charitable and civic organizations because we all benefit so much from being a part of this community."

As for the future, Joyner sees Prudential C. Dan Joyner Realtors continuing to be respected in the community as it grows with honesty and integrity. ⌐

Ashmore Bros., Inc.

In 1930, Russell C. Ashmore Sr. began a landscape, grading, and surface treatment company with a Mack chain-drive truck, a pick, and two shovels. Twelve years later, Ashmore's brother, Mack A. Ashmore joined as a partner and the company was named Ashmore Bros., Inc.

The brothers purchased their first asphalt paver in 1942 and located a hot-mix plant on Stone Avenue near downtown Greenville. Business picked up, and Ashmore Bros. began landing commercial contracts to pave parking lots and roads.

Through the years, Ashmore Bros. has experienced steady growth in product scope as well as size. Today, the company has 200 employees and serves the entire Upstate with asphalt plants in Greer and Anderson. Ashmore Bros. has also built a stable of heavy machinery and equipment that is state-of-the-art.

The philosophy that has always driven Ashmore Bros. has been quality work at a reasonable cost, says Russell C. Ashmore, Jr., Vice President of Research and Development. "We strive to exceed the required specifications on all of our jobs, because repeat business is the best business," Ashmore says.

Ashmore joined the company in 1960, and his brother Richard Ashmore, who serves as the company's president, joined a year earlier.

The company is not only recognized for asphalt construction, but also for professional site work performed by their own forces, consisting of grading storm drainage, advanced slip-form curb and gutters, "in-place" asphalt recycling, and laser technology.

Ashmore said the company attempts to maintain a balance between work it does for the private and public sectors. Ashmore Bros. has worked on projects for the South Carolina Department of Transportation (SCDOT), BMW, Michelin, Haywood Mall, Fluor Daniel, Thornblade, and Patewood Plaza, just to name a few.

The company became the first contractor in South Carolina to successfully build a highway using slip-form curb and gutter construction by completing the section of Haywood Road between Pelham Road and East North Street. The technology has also been utilized by Ashmore Bros. in subdivisions and shopping centers as well as industrial site construction.

Another project of note is Duke Power's Bad Creek development in northern Oconee County near the North Carolina line. Despite rugged terrain and steep grades, the company successfully completed the project on schedule using in-place recycling techniques. "We pride ourselves in tackling tough jobs many companies shy away from," Ashmore said.

Technologies such as in-place asphalt recycling and laser technology have enabled Ashmore clients to realize cost savings and unmatched accuracy on their projects.

In 1996, Ashmore Brothers received a letter of commendation from the SCDOT, for a resurfacing project on I-26 in which the company surpassed the department's requirements for smoothness.

Ashmore said he believes the company has played a significant role in the development and growth of Greenville and the Upstate. Along the way, Ashmore Bros. has given back to the community by making "in-kind" contributions to civic and charitable organizations.

As for the future of Ashmore Bros., it's in good hands, according to Ashmore. His two sons, Mark and Greg, and Richard's sons, David and Rick, who all serve as vice presidents, will lead the company in the years to come.

Pictured together are the three generations of Ashmore's who have continued to represent their family owned business for the past 67 years. Seated (l-r): Richard Ashmore, Mack Ashmore, Russell Ashmore Jr. Standing (l-r): Mark Ashmore, Rick Ashmore, Greg Ashmore, David Ashmore.

Robinson Company of Greenville, Inc.

*T*he Robinson family has been a part of Greenville since the early nineteen hundreds and has been an integral part of its development from a small textile village to the thriving metropolitan area it is today. Their faith in and love for Greenville is demonstrated daily in their contributions to its economic development and its quality of life.

Helping Greenville grow has been a priority of the Robinson Company for more than 75 years. Through the years, Pat Haskell-Robinson, James Robinson, and Corbin Haskell have been focused on the future of Greenville. Serving as Chairman of the Board of the Greenville Chamber of Commerce in 1995 is one of many positions Mrs. Robinson has held in the community.

Since the company began, a significant portion of the business has been from the Appraisal Division. It is one of the largest real estate appraisal organizations in South Carolina with eight appraisal associates, five of whom are members of the Appraisal Institute, four with MAI designations, and two with the SRA designation. Corbin Haskell, MAI, serves as Vice President of the company, while James Robinson, MAI, is Chairman of the Board. Mr. Robinson has served as the Vice Chairman of the South Carolina Appraiser Board, President of the South Carolina Appraisal Chapter, and President of the Clemson University Real Estate Foundation. Robinson appraisers have performed commercial, industrial, and residential appraisal assignments throughout the Southeast and are qualified to perform appraisals for financial institutions and

governmental agencies as well as private interests.

When BMW decided to locate its first North American manufacturing plant in the Upstate, the Robinson Company wanted to play an active role in making it happen. Marian Graham, Director of the Corporate Relocation Division of Robinson Company, led the way by putting together a consortium of corporate relocation directors from Greenville and Spartanburg real estate companies to help meet BMW's extensive needs. Since that time the Robinson Company has been involved in international real estate and continues to enjoy a productive relationship with BMW. Additionally, the relocation division services a variety of international and national corporate accounts in the Greenville area, and a number of relocation management companies who represent Greenville based clients.

The Residential Sales Division of Robinson Company specializes in the listing and sale of middle and upper income housing. From helping first time home buyers to the most sophisticated purchaser, Mrs. Robinson, who serves as

Corbin Haksell, Executive Vice president; Patricia Haskell-Robinson, President & CEO; James Robinson, Chairman of the Board; Marian Graham, Vice President Corporate Development.

President, CEO, and Broker in Charge, states that "The company is dedicated to providing the highest quality of personalized professional service—a distinguishing hallmark of the Robinson Company. Whether from the Upstate or another part of the world, they are very important to us."

In a time when real estate companies are merging and franchising with national networks, the Robinson Company remains one of Greenville's prominent independent brokers. Although it is not the goal of the company to be the largest, it is their goal to provide a level of service second to none.

American Equipment Company

Go back far enough into the family tree of American Equipment Company (AMECO), one of the world's largest equipment and project services companies, and you will find that their roots began in Greenville. The company originally known as the Daniel Equipment Division, founded in 1947, was incorporated into American Equipment in 1971. Headquartered on Anderson Road in Greenville, the company has become one of the top five equipment suppliers in the United States and now has operations in Canada, Puerto Rico, Mexico, Chile, Venezuela, Argentina, Peru, Indonesia, the Philippines, China, and Australia. AMECO has grown into a global service company with a strong commitment to safety, innovation, and customer focus.

With 10 consecutive years of growth, AMECO has recently utilized two strategies to ensure continued growth—globalization and acquisitions. AMECO has 64 locations in 12 countries, with a leadership position in providing construction equipment, maintenance, tools, and related services to clients and projects around the globe. "Latin America continues to be a strong market for us, with a particular focus on Peru, Chile, Venezuela, and Argentina," said Gary Bernardez,

The American Equipment management team stands ready to serve (left to right): Gary Bernardez, Bill Traylor, Charles Snyder, John McAleer, Bruce Jackson, and John Malone.

Director, Global Business Development. "Our ability to work closely with clients to develop a customized package of products and services to meet their specific needs is a key competence that we will continue to leverage."

AMECO has completed five key acquisitions within the past three years to expand product lines and geographic coverage in the North American market. Acquisitions include S&R Equipment in the Midwest; SMA Equipment Company and SMA Information Systems in California; Stith Equipment in Georgia; J.W Burress, Inc. in Virginia, North Carolina, and Maryland; and MAPSA in Mexico. "Our representation has grown with the best names in the equipment industry," noted President Charles Snyder. "Our dealerships represent premium product lines such as Grove Worldwide, Komatsu, Hitachi, JLG, Ingersoll-Rand, J.I. Case, Link-Belt, Terex, and many others."

AMECO continues to create value for customers by listening to their needs and providing services to improve their business success. AMECO's Fleet Services, for example, assists clients in focusing on their core business by assuming responsibility for all aspects of their equipment operations. This approach improves clients' cash flow and reduces operating expenses while shifting fixed costs to variable, thereby adding flexibility to their operations.

American Equipment Puerto Rico office. spells out the safety message.

American Equipment project in Argentina.

AMECO provides clients with the most modern equipment, the latest technology, and develops equipment plans outlining exactly when and what equipment will be needed for a particular task. AMECO offers a detailed economic analysis to determine the most cost-effective method for the client to procure equipment via rental, purchase, or lease. Other services include financing, program management, and a comprehensive preventive maintenance program to ensure optimum equipment availability and reliability. AMECO's ISO 9002 certification demonstrates a high level of commitment to quality.

A key component of AMECO's success has been an emphasis on safety. The company is dedicated to the concept that all accidents are preventable. This philosophy has enabled AMECO to win three National Safety Council records.

Safety remains a cornerstone of the AMECO vision: "We are the largest and most effective global provider of construction and industrial equipment and project-related services. Our entrepreneurial, empowered, quality-driven culture holds safety as a primary mandate."

147

12

Chapter Twelve

Business and Finance

Greater Greenville Chamber of Commerce

Mention the Greater Greenville Chamber of Commerce, and you may get a wide variety of responses on what purpose it serves.

It's the first place to turn for information when making the decision to move to the Greenville area.

It's Greenville County's advocate for economic development.

It's the voice of the business community in the governing halls of Columbia.

It's a business news source.

It's a promoter of small business and entrepreneurship.

It's the place to be for networking and training.

It rallies for a better-educated work force.

The fact is, the Greenville Chamber is all those things . . . and more.

Economic Development

Take a look at Greenville's business landscape, and chances are that the Chamber has had some hand in each company's presence here—whether through direct recruitment or simply as an information source. Throughout its 119-year history, the Chamber has helped generate capital investment and new jobs for the Greenville community. The Chamber's Economic Development arm supports the regions economic and tax base by recruiting new businesses as well as aiding the already established companies who already claim Greenville as home. Its goal is simple: to ensure that Greenville maintains a secure economy by creating a diversified base of businesses for the area.

Small Business

More than 80 percent of the Chamber's membership is made up of businesses with 50 or fewer employees. The Chamber provides many services aimed to aid the small business community such as training programs and minority business development. Through its signature program, BuyUpstate, the Small Business department of the Chamber promotes local purchasing through matching buyers and suppliers.

Workforce Development

The Chamber not only works to bring quality businesses to Greenville, but also to fill those businesses with qualified workers. Through its Workforce Development department, the Chamber partners with public schools, technical schools, local colleges, and universities in an effort to identify employer needs and train and increase opportunities for current and potential employees.

Communications

The Chamber provides the business community with a myriad of publications offering inside information on economic development, legislation, work force development, and the important issues that affect their bottom line and the way they live. From its award-winning monthly business magazine, *Outlook,* to its newest publication, *Insight,* a faxed bi-weekly newsletter, the Chamber is the essential resource for Greenville's business news.

Membership

The Chamber's membership represents the movers and shakers of Greenville—from Fortune 500 companies to single employee operations. The organization works toward offering its members a variety of benefits and special events such as the golf tournament, Annual Meeting, Inter-Community Visit and Business After Hours, and discounts from Chamber-member companies. There are more than 30 committees in which members can become involved—committees which deal with such issues as legislation, minority business, education, and infrastructure needs.

While the Greater Greenville Chamber wears many hats, all of its facets have one common goal: to promote the quality development of Upstate South Carolina through balanced growth, service to members and the public, and a community-wide approach to the issues shaping the region's future. It's a goal the organization has had for 119 years and one it will carry on into the next century. ◙

Wachovia Bank

Wachovia Bank, N.A. is a member of Wachovia Corporation, an interstate bank holding company with dual headquarters in Winston-Salem, North Carolina and Atlanta, Georgia. The bank serves regional, national, and international markets. Its member companies offer credit and deposit services, insurance, investment, and trust products and information services to consumers and to corporations, both in and outside the United States. Consumer products and services are provided through a network of retail branches, ATMs, Wachovia On-Call 24-hour telephone banking, automated Phone Access, and Internet-based investing and banking at www.wachovia.com. In addition, Wachovia serves consumers

Wachovia Bank's Upstate Managers are (left to right): Dixon Harrill, Charles Eldridge, John Haas, Richard Schweitzer, Kevin Short, Karen Litchfield, David Beard, David Parker, and Judy Tucker.

nationwide through its credit card business. Wachovia provides global solutions to corporate clients through locations in Chicago, London, New York, and Sao Paulo; through representatives in Hong Kong and Tokyo; and through worldwide strategic alliances.

Wachovia has more than 700 offices in the Carolinas, Georgia, and Virginia. An additional 39 offices joined the network in the spring of 1998 when bank mergers in Florida were completed. Greenville is home to 14 Wachovia offices with more than 225 employees providing a broad range of financial services.

Wachovia currently ranks 17th in the nation among bank holding companies, as measured by assets of more than $65 billion on December 31, 1997. On the same date, the bank also ranked 15th with a total market capitalization of $16.7 billion. In 1996, *U.S. Banker* magazine ranked Wachovia the best-performing

bank in the country among banks with assets exceeding $25 billion. Wachovia Investments ranked second in an audit of 40 of the nation's largest bank-affiliated brokerage programs conducted between October and December of 1997 by San Francisco-based PROPHET Market Research, an independent marketing consulting firm.

Since its founding in 1879 Wachovia has been a pacesetter in meeting the financial needs and public interests of the communities in which it operates. The bank is a leader in banking technologies, for example, Wachovia On-Call was South Carolina's first 24-hour telephone banking center. Wachovia offers a range of products and services geared to meet the changing financial needs of its markets, and to meet customers' changing needs. One such service is Profitable Relationship Optimization (PRO), which is an integrated relationship management strategy employing information, technology, and local market sales execution to permit the proactive contacting of targeted customers with suggested services. Wachovia also is a corporate leader, committed to efforts to improve quality of life through such areas as education, healthcare, economic and community development, and the arts.

Wachovia has a proud and distinguished history of service in South Carolina since 1834. In the Greenville area in 1926, Norwood National Bank of Greenville and a Columbia bank merged with the Bank of Charleston, the state's oldest financial institution, to form South Carolina National Bank. After serving the Greenville community for 65 years, SCN merged with Wachovia in 1991. The tradition of service continues through Wachovia's superior financial service and exemplary corporate citizenship. Wachovia and its employees are committed to the Greenville market and are actively involved in civic, community, and humanitarian organizations to sustain the great quality of life in Upstate South Carolina. ◘

BellSouth

The world of telecommunications is changing every day. Today it's cellular phones, digital pagers, and Internet access, but tomorrow will present a whole new host of technological advances that will make staying in touch even easier.

Although it's hard to say what products and services will be available in the future, one thing is for sure: BellSouth will be right there leading the way.

The possibilities in telecommunications are endless. One wave of the future, according to Arnold Burrell, regional director with BellSouth, is the bundling of services that will include all or most of a customer's needs wrapped into one convenient package. Long-distance, local service, Internet access, and wireless communications will all be available from the same provider.

Other conveniences will be transferable phone numbers. For instance, if a family moves from one side of town to the other where the exchange is different, they will be able to take their phone number with them, according to Burrell.

The telecommunications industry has come a long way through the years, as has BellSouth since it began providing services in Greenville on May 21, 1882. The company began with 16 crank-type telephones and several young men employed as operators. Today, BellSouth has about

450 employees in Greenville and the surrounding area.

BellSouth opened its initial operation on Laurens Street and has relocated several times in the downtown area to accommodate its growth. The company is currently located at 218 College Street in a multi-story building, which has recently undergone more than $2 million in renovations and architectural improvements.

In the future, it's inevitable that the telecommunications industry will undergo many changes, which will lead to the implementation of new regulations by the Federal Communications Commission (FCC). Many of the new regulations will allow for new providers to enter regional markets where competition has been minimal or non-existent in the past.

"It will be a challenge for BellSouth as new competition enters the marketplace," Burrell says. "However, we're confident we will remain the premiere provider of telecommunications services in the Upstate because of our dedicated staff of employees who have the experience and know-how to handle any obstacle thrown their way."

Burrell stresses the importance of BellSouth's involvement in the community. "When competitors enter the market here, they may or may not have the community involvement that we have," he says.

BellSouth has been an integral part of the

community for a long time and that trend will continue. Whether its supporting the Chamber of Commerce or the United Way, the YMCA or the local arts council through contributions and volunteerism, BellSouth's community involvement is an investment in the future of the Upstate.

BellSouth is a $21 billion communications services company. It provides telecommunications, wireless communications, directory advertising and publishing, video, Internet, and information services to more than 30 million customers in 20 countries worldwide.

Carolina First

"Greenville gave us our start," recalls Mack I. Whittle, Jr., President and CEO of Carolina First Corporation. "It had a deep, entrepreneurial current that we were able to tap into. Today, that current is stronger than ever. This is a city crackling with ideas and energy."

In many ways, the growth of the bank parallels the growth of the city. Founded here in 1986, Carolina First Corporation is today the largest independent bank holding company in South Carolina with assets in excess of $2.2 billion and 65 banking offices throughout the state, ten of which are located in the Greenville area.

Carolina First offers a full spectrum of banking services through a variety of delivery systems including telephone, grocery store, workplace, and PC-based banking. Other services are provided through subsidiaries: Carolina First Mortgage Company—the second largest mortgage loan servicer in South Carolina, Blue Ridge Finance Company, and CF

Getting a loan is now as easy as making a cash withdrawal from an ATM.

Investment Company— a small business investment company.

Carolina First has seen remarkable growth with assets, loans, and deposits showing growth at compound rates in excess of 20 percent per year over the bank's lifetime. Carolina First now has more than 6 percent of the total banking market in South Carolina and ranks sixth in total deposit market share.

Carolina First owes this growth in part to its position as a *super community bank* aimed at serving individuals and small-to medium-sized businesses. *Putting customers first* is the bank's stated goal. Winning and keeping customers through flexible and creative banking relationships is the result.

"When we see a need we respond," explains Mr. Whittle. As an example, the international department was started in response to a number of the bank's small business clients who found themselves for the first time doing business overseas. Mr. Whittle concedes that it's unusual to have international banking expertise in an operation the size of Carolina First, but he says, "We didn't hesitate."

Like Greenville itself, Carolina First doesn't shrink from change and the opportunities it provides. For instance, Carolina First holds common stock of both Affinity Technology Group, Inc., a developer of automated lending technologies, and *NetB@nk,* Inc., one of the first on-line, real-time Internet banks. Naturally, at the bottom of this interest in technology is the bank's desire to understand and serve its customers better.

Carolina First was created in 1986 with one simple yet bold mission: to become South Carolina's premier bank by putting customers first.

Part of that service involves the reinvestment of local funds into South Carolina communities. Carolina First has received several "outstanding" ratings (highest ranking) under federal community reinvestment regulations. Additionally, in 1998, the bank was recognized as the top producer in South Carolina for the "Main Street Investment Program," a program designed to promote the growth of existing small businesses and assist in the start-up of new businesses.

Underscoring an abiding commitment to Greenville, Carolina First was pivotal in the 1998 South Main Street revitalization and development package that included renovation of the historic Poinsett Hotel, a new city parking garage, and its own new ten-story office tower—the first addition to the city's skyline in over a decade.

HomeGold Financial, Inc.™

The tenacious and persistent attitude of the rhinoceros embodies the corporate philosophy of HomeGold Financial, Inc.™ (HGFI™). As the company's corporate symbol, the rhino serves as a reminder to take charge and find success in the business jungle.

HGFI is a diversified financial services company headquartered in Greenville that originates, services, securitizes, and sells residential mortgage loans and small business loans. The company makes substantially all of its loans to borrowers who have limited access to credit or who may be considered credit-impaired by conventional lending standards.

HGFI was founded in 1990 when Greenville businessmen Jack Sterling, Buck Mickel, Tommy Wyche, and Tee Hooper purchased controlling interest in NRUC Corporation. In 1991, the company purchased Carolina Investors, Inc., Premier Financial Services, and Loan Pro$. In 1992, the name of the company was changed to Emergent Group Inc. and Emergent Business Capital (EBC), the commercial lending division, was formed. EBC has expanded with the formation of Emergent Equity Advisors, Inc. and Emergent Financial Corp. which provide

mezzanine financing and asset-based revolving loans to small businesses.

In the Upstate, EBC has originated loans to 46 businesses totaling $22.3 million to help with start-up costs, renovations, refinancing, and acquisitions. Some recognizable businesses in this group include Vince's Enterprises, Inc., Hurley & Harrison, Inc., Kyrus Corporation, Trios, Hampton Inn, and Greenville Racquet and Fitness Club.

Between 1992 and 1997, total loan originations grew from $57 million to $1.2 billion per year. During the same period, employee growth was also brisk. In 1992, HGFI employed 40 people in the Upstate. By the end of 1997, the company had grown to 716 employees in the Upstate and 623 others across the country.

HGFI's mortgage division accounts for nearly 85 percent of the company's loan originations. The company's mortgage lending operation has grown through wholesale and retail channels. In 1996, Emergent began retail mortgage loan operations under the trade name HomeGold®. To help associates carry out the mortgage group's mission, the REAL REWARDS® program was developed and implemented to counsel borrowers on reducing or eliminating their personal debt. The company also adopted the slogan "The Power to be Debt Free™."

HGFI's vision includes improving the community. Education is a top contribution priority as evidenced through the annual presentation of the Dwight A. Holder Scholarship and donations to the S.C. Governor's School for the Arts, The Peace Center, and Greenville Tech.

HomeGold Financial, Inc. associates also approach their community involvement with a hard charging and determined attitude—like the rhino. HGFI has been recognized by March of Dimes and United Way for its participation in their fundraising campaigns. The company also supports other community improvement efforts, including Junior Achievement and Urban League. In 1997, HGFI proudly accepted the Better Business Bureau's Golden Torch Award which recognized the

HomeGold Financial, Inc. Principal Officers: (l to r) Robert S. Davis, Vice President—Administration; Kevin J. Mast, Vice President, Chief Financial Officer and Treasurer; John M. "Jack" Sterling Jr., Chairman of the Board and Chief Executive Officer; and Keith B. Giddens, President and Chief Operating Officer.

company's commitment to ethics and integrity above all else.

During the summer of 1998, shareholders approved changing the company name to HomeGold Financial, Inc., and the company opened its new mortgage and data operations center on Pelham Road. The 107,000 square-foot facility, which represents an $8 million capital investment in the Greenville community, houses approximately 600 associates.

The future for HomeGold Financial, Inc. looks bright as the company plans to charge ahead and bring 450 to 500 new jobs to the Upstate over the next five years. ◖

Emergent Business Capital Officers: (l to r) Capers Easterby, President of EBC Equity Group; Susan Streich, President of EBC SBA Group; Connie Warne, President of EBC Asset-Based Lending Group; and Sam Couvillion, Chief Executive Officer.

HomeGold, Inc. Officers: (seated) Wade Hall, Executive Vice President of Strategic Development; Kim Bullard, Executive Vice President of Servicing: and Joe Rutter, Senior Vice President/National Sales Manager–Retail Division. (standing) Laird Minor, Executive Vice President of Structured Finance; Ron Boiter, Senior Vice President/National Sales Manager–Wholesale Division; Dennis Canupp, President and Chief Operating Officer; and Mark Keegan, Group General Counsel and Executive Vice President of Quality Management.

Piedmont Travel, Inc.

What does it take to build one of the largest travel management firms in the entire United States? "Hard work and good people," answers Bob Townes, founder of Piedmont Travel, Inc. A banker by trade, Bob saw an opportunity in 1976 when he looked at the books of a small, Greenville travel agency. At the time, the company employed three people, booked all reservations over the phone, and hand-wrote its airline tickets or printed them via teletype machine. Today, Piedmont Travel employs 75 agents and support staff, is fully computerized, boasts annual sales of $51 million, and is the largest travel agency in South Carolina. In fact, it is the 95th largest travel management firm in the country. Quite an achievement for a local business!

"It's really no secret," say his sons, John and Scott, who now run the business since Bob's retirement in 1994. "Our father taught us that to make a business work, you had to locate and hire good people, treat them with dignity and respect, and provide them with a working environment in which they are appreciated and can grow. If you're successful at doing that, the rest should take care of itself." Evidently that philosophy has paid off, as Piedmont is well recognized within the community as a travel powerhouse.

Piedmont Travel provides a full array of travel services for all of its clients, but their strength and focus is in business travel. However, with department

specialists in corporate, vacation, group, and meeting planning travel they are able to take care of virtually any travel need that may present itself. All of the services that they provide are performed in-house from their Greenville headquarters, which gives them quite an advantage over their competition. "From a competitive stand-point, no one in our market can match our combination of local service and world-wide coverage," says Scott. "By providing these services in-house, we are able to maintain a high level of control and personal attention, which is impossible for 'mega' travel agencies to provide. In addition, we meet face-to-face with our clients to review results and make suggestions for cost-savings, and this intense level of service and attention is hard to duplicate by national firms."

"Greenville is a vibrant and growing community," says John, "And we are both fortu-nate and proud to have participated in some of this growth over the past 22

Piedmont Travel is a growing family run business passed on from father to sons. (l-r) John Townes, Bob Townes, founder of Piedmont Travel, and Scott Townes.

years." In fact, the area has seen many changes since the Townes family settled here, as their Greenville roots go back to well before the Civil War. "Part of the pride we feel is due to the fact that our family has participated in Greenville's growth since its founding in the early 1800s. We feel a deep sense of belonging here and feel obligated to give something back to the community that has been so good to us." This feeling is evident in that all of the Townes are or have been active in many local organizations, including the United Way, the YMCA, the American Heart Association, the Sertoma Club, and the American Cancer Society. "We plan to have a presence in this area for many years to come and can only hope that we will be able to instill these values in our own children," state John and Scott. "Again, this is a lesson that we learned from our father."

Piedmont Travel, Inc. is located in Greenville, South Carolina.

13

Chapter Thirteen

Health Care and Education

159

Greenville Hospital System

As you look at the beautiful sights around Greenville, you may not think about how the quality of health care adds to the quality of life. Yet, health care is a vital part of every community and something that touches the life of every person. What you'll find in Greenville is South Carolina's leading health system, nationally recognized for its clinical advances, research, and medical education. Welcome to the Greenville Hospital System.

GHS is recognized as the region's quality care leader by the National Research Corporation, an organization that ranks health systems across the country based on consumer preference. GHS is the only health care provider to receive this award in the Upstate and has received this designation annually since it was first awarded in this area. This level of quality care, combined with an extensive range and depth of services, fosters a quality of life that rivals many major metropolitan areas and is a source of pride for more than 7,500 health care professionals employed by GHS.

Located in the growth corridor between Charlotte and Atlanta, Greenville is nestled in the piedmont of the Blue Ridge Mountains. Such geographic advantages,

A teaching, research, and regional referral center, Greenville Hospital System is a leader in bringing clinical advancements, new procedures, and advanced technology to the area.

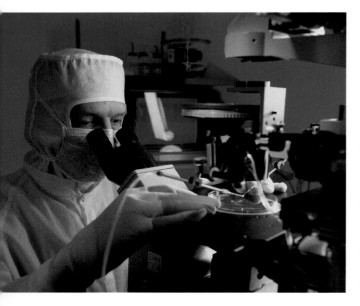

combined with forward-thinking leadership, transformed this small upcountry village into a dynamic and diverse city that draws people and businesses from around the world. Greenville Hospital System's roots reach back more than 100 years to the beginning of its mission to serve the community.

What started in the late 1800s as a Women's Auxiliary project to provide health care to the people of Greenville led to the opening of the city's first public hospital in 1912. Over the years, the hospital expanded to meet the area's increasing health needs and became one of the largest, most advanced health care systems in the country. In fact, GHS developed from a visionary plan that pioneered the multi-hospital system concept during the 1950s when it formed the nation's first health system. This model served as a national standard for health care delivery.

Today, the system includes Allen Bennett Hospital in Greer, Greenville Memorial Hospital near downtown Greenville, Hillcrest Hospital in Simpsonville, and North Greenville Hospital outpatient center in Travelers Rest. GHS also offers a comprehensive range of specialized health care facilities, home health and occupational health services, transitional care and nursing home care, a primary care physician network, a health plan affiliate, and a 24-hour health information service.

Greenville Hospital System's services and resources, combined with its teaching and research activities, keep the system at the forefront of health care delivery. GHS has teaching affiliations with several institutions of higher learning, including the University of South Carolina School of

Greenville Memorial Hospital is one of three free-standing hospitals that provides convenient access to health services throughout the Greenville area. The lobby provides a relaxing setting for patients and visitors to enjoy.

Medicine and the Medical University of South Carolina, and a biomedical research affiliation with Clemson University. These partnerships and the outstanding medical and clinical staff who support them ensure clinical expertise and availability of advanced procedures and treatments.

The hospital system also provides specialized services to care for individual health needs. These programs are supported by a network that provides convenient access to all aspects of care, including:

•**Emergency Services** - providing the most extensive emergency services in the Upstate with a county-wide network of four emergency rooms, including Greenville's only Level I Trauma Center and Children's Emergency Center, as well as convenient Urgent Treatment Centers for extended hours care.

•**Behavioral Health Services** - providing comprehensive, individualized treatment for children, adolescents, and adults.

•**Cancer Treatment Center** - combining

Comprehensive services, clinical expertise, and unique programs, such as the Children's Emergency Center, make Greenville Hospital System the health care provider of choice in the Upstate.

complete medical, surgical, and radiation treatment with prevention, diagnosis, clinical, and bench research.

•**Center for Women** - providing comprehensive services ranging from OB-GYN and maternity to the highest level of subspecialty care, education, and support.

•**The Children's Hospital** - offering a full range of sophisticated pediatric services, featuring 31 subspecialties. The Children's Hospital provides the area's only Children's Emergency Center, which is designed, staffed, and equipped for the special needs of children; Greenville's only Level III Neonatal Intensive Care Unit; a Pediatric Intensive Care Unit; certified school-based health education; and the state's first day treatment center for medically fragile children.

•**Heart Institute** - South Carolina's largest and most experienced cardiac center, offering diagnosis, prevention, treatment, and HeartLife®, one of the leading cardiac rehabilitation programs in the nation.

•**Roger C. Peace Rehabilitation Hospital** - featuring full-service inpatient and

outpatient care for brain and spinal cord injuries, strokes, amputations, and orthopaedic injuries.

Greenville Hospital System is renowned for its advanced medical technology,

comprehensive services, and modern facilities, but its true strength comes from people—knowledgeable and compassionate doctors, nurses, clinical specialists, volunteers, and other health care professionals who work together to care for people who call the Upstate home. ⏎

Greenville Hospital System is proud of its history of service to the people of the Upstate. This historical display recounts the system's 100-year history and commitment to improving health in the community.

Bob Jones University

*T*he history of Bob Jones University in Greenville spans back more than 50 years when, in 1947, the campus relocated to this city from its previous home in Cleveland, Tennessee.

The Founder's Memorial Amphitorium is the central part of campus life. Chapel, attended daily by all students, and a vast majority of other events are held here.

Dr. Bob Jones, a well-known evangelist, founded the university in 1927 in College Point, Florida on the basis of encouraging the highest academic standards—a simple philosophy that also emphasized the importance of culture and a down-to-earth, practical Christian philosophy of self-control that was both orthodox and fervent in its evangelistic spirit.

Jonathan Pait, Community Relations Coordinator for Bob Jones University, said that in 1946, the university came within only minutes of locating its campus in Knoxville, Tennessee. However, a woman who was reluctant to sell her property and an opportunistic realtor in Greenville greatly influenced the relocation of the university.

"There were many factors involved in locating the university in Greenville, but most importantly, Dr. Jones felt this was where the Lord wanted us to be," Pait said.

Since holding its first classes in the fall of 1947, Bob Jones University has grown in facilities, enrollment, and scope. Today, more than 150 undergraduate and graduate majors are offered to an annual enrollment of more than 5,000 students. The university's main entrance is located on Wade Hampton Boulevard, and the campus is situated on 225 acres within the city limits of Greenville.

While the university has continued to grow, the philosophy and religious beliefs have not changed. "We believe whatever the Bible says is so," Pait said. "We believe in making our lifestyles fit the Scriptures."

Throughout the years, Bob Jones University has turned out many leaders in the business and political communities of Greenville. "Bob Jones University has helped build a solid base of honest, hardworking citizens in the community," Pait said.

"We like to think that Bob Jones University has given Greenville a community with a sense of family atmosphere, generated through a tradition of conservative philosophy toward life," Pait said.

Six different schools comprise the University: the College of Arts and Science, the School of Religion, the School of Fine Arts, the School of Education, the School of Business Administration, and the School of Applied Sciences.

Some of the main features on the university's campus include the Mack Library, which offers seating to over 1,500 students, contains more than 225,000 volumes and regularly receives more than 1,000 periodicals. The newly renovated Howell Memorial Science Building contains laboratories for biology, chemistry, physics, and electronics, as well as a computer science lab. The Fine Arts Building contains studios for music and art instruction, in addition to practice halls for orchestra, band, chorus, and musical ensembles. The Radio and Television Broadcasting department facilities are also housed in the Fine Arts Building, as are the Music Library and several classrooms.

One of the highlights of the campus is the University Art Gallery and Museum, which has been proclaimed the "greatest collection of religious art in the Western hemisphere."

Bob Jones University also offers an educational program on grade levels K-12, which provides a strong character-building emphasis through training in discipline and a thorough saturation with Biblical principles. The curriculum is well-balanced and academically stimulating, thus providing a solid foundation for those choosing to further their education. ◗

The quiet atmosphere of campus life at Bob Jones University allows students to concentrate on their studies as well as relax in the peaceful surroundings.

St. Francis Health System

*I*n 1932, the Franciscan Sisters of the Poor arrived in Greenville to operate the city's first private, not-for-profit hospital. Today, St. Francis Health System has grown with two hospital facilities, outpatient services, home care, philanthropic foundation, physician division, and benefits network that provides quality, cost-effective care to Upstate residents.

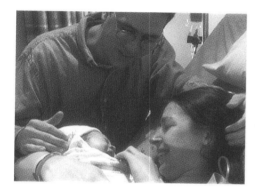

St. Francis Women's and Family Hospital has a family-centered birthing program.

The system continues the Sisters' mission to care for those less fortunate. In 1997, St. Francis contributed $18 million in quantifiable benefits to the poor and underprivileged across the Upstate.

St. Francis Hospital in the downtown area, and St. Francis Women's and Family Hospital on the city's growing east side, offer 24-hour emergency care, plus medical, surgical, and critical care services.

St. Francis Hospital is a 257-bed medical center that also provides cardiac catheterization, Louis P. Batson Jr. Cancer Care Center, comprehensive radiology services, transitional care, outpatient services, and an inpatient physical rehabilitation center. A $6 million cardiovascular surgery center will open in December 1998.

St. Francis Women's and Family Hospital includes acute care and critical care services for men, women, and children, in addition to a 24-hour emergency department. The 62-bed hospital also provides comprehensive women's care, including gynecology obstetrics, Level II neonatology, and mammography services.

St. Francis offers the Emmanuel Unit, a 12-bed inpatient area that combines the spiritual aspects of healing with medical care and treatment. The Emmanuel Unit is a Christian-focused unit, but patients of all faiths and beliefs are welcome.

St. Francis Hospital HomeCare meets the needs of patients who need help from clinicians, but may not need the comprehensive services of a hospital. Services include skilled and private duty nursing, physical, speech, occupational, infusion therapies, and medical equipment. Hospice, which helps patients and their families cope with terminal illness, is also available.

St. Francis is part of the Franciscan Health Partnership Inc., Albany, NY. The system sponsors more than 400 programs for the poor and general community, plus hospitals, long-term care facilities, home health agencies, and community services in five states. Each affiliated system is governed by a local board of directors.

The commitment by the administration and staff of St. Francis facilities has yielded patient satisfaction scores consistently ranking among the highest in the nation for similar facilities. Additionally, St. Francis Hospital has the shortest lengths of stay for selected diagnoses for patients in Greenville County and the lowest post-hospitalization complication rates of any Greenville County hospital.

St. Francis Health System is the only provider in the Upstate to utilize the Iameter clinical information system. This high-tech information tool helps manage costs without damaging quality of care, or reducing patient satisfaction.

St. Francis' Continuous Quality Improvement (CQI) program allows teams of employees and physicians to work together to ensure that every component of patient care and facilities operation is as efficient as possible. CQI teams pay attention to everything from surgical procedures to how supplies are purchased.

St. Francis' Optimum Health Network physician-hospital organization is available to insurance companies, employers, and third-party payors. The network includes approximately 400 physicians and all St. Francis Health System facilities, plus Charter Greenville Behavioral Health Systems psychiatric and substance abuse treatment facility; Atlanta's Piedmont Hospital; St. Joseph's Heart Institute in Atlanta, a nationally-recognized regional center of excellence for cardiovascular surgery; and Mayo Clinic Jacksonville.

Optimum offers a preferred provider network, risk-bearing network, utilization review, workers' compensation services, and occupational health programs. Optimum serves as the umbrella company for these services. Its purpose is to give its network members health insurance options that allow employers of all sizes to select cost-effective, high-quality health care delivery systems.

Optimum Health Network has more than 70,000 members and is one of the largest managed care networks in Greenville.

SaintLine™, the free St. Francis physician referal service, allows callers to select physicians practicing throughout the Upstate area.

The St. Francis Foundation is the philanthropic arm of St. Francis. Funds raised by the foundation are used for care for the indigent, construction and renovation, purchase of high-tech equipment, and community services. The foundation also offers tax-advantaged giving and estate planning services. 🔲

St. Francis Health System provides high-tech surgical care at two hospitals and an outpatient center.

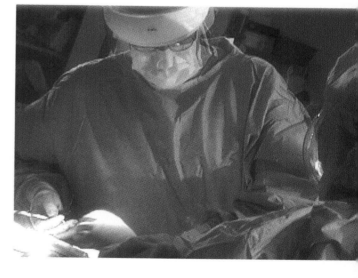

ZCI Integrated Solutions, Corp.

ZCI Integrated Solutions, Corp. the first managed care company in South Carolina focusing exclusively on workers' compensation management, brings innovation to managing occupational injuries for the state's employers. With the highest level of professionalism, a meticulous attention to detail, and aggressive management beginning just minutes after an injury occurs, ZCI reduces costs associated with workplace injuries. ZCI expedites the entire post-injury process so that employees receive quality care and are able to get back to work as soon as medically admissable. In the process, employers avoid the hassle and significantly reduce costs associated with occupational injuries.

With highly-credentialed professionals, ZCI successfully manages the three components of workers' compensation—administration, medical management, and case closure—allowing participating companies to realize significant cost savings. Covering the entire spectrum of injuries from minor injuries to serious traumas, ZCI helps companies take charge of workers' compensation by serving as a liaison between employers, employees, health care providers, and insurance companies during the aftermath of an occupational injury.

Within 15 minutes of a work-related injury, the ZCI clinical staff immediately intervenes, and the system of managed care begins as the medical professionals make sure that employees receive the necessary medical care in a cost-efficient manner. "ZCI coordinates quality, cost-effective care, and efficiently handles workers' compensation claims so that employers and employees fully understand all dimensions of care, recovery, and claim status," said ZCI President and CEO Dr. Richard A. Matula.

Matula, along with ZCI's co-founder Michael R. West, ZCI's Vice-President of Business Development and Planning, moved the company headquarters to Greenville, South Carolina in 1996 after extensive research indicated a demand for the unique managed care service. "We received numerous invitations from the Greater Greenville Chamber of Commerce to join the business community and in retrospect we are delighted that we chose to establish our headquarters in Greenville," Matula said.

Today, ZCI services numerous companies in a variety of different industries, putting the well-established managed care principles to work for companies throughout the state. "Workers' compensation managed care has been successfully embraced by companies in the Northeast and West Coast, and now ZCI allows South Carolina businesses to have the same benefit," West said.

ZCI's managed care services encompass an integrated medical delivery system and an efficient communications system, so that employees will receive seamless care and employers can effectively monitor progress of injured workers. ZCI has formed strategic partnerships with health care facilities across the state to provide care for injured employees. The company continues to expand the preferred provider network by forming relationships with physicians, specialists, hospitals, and other medical institutions.

With early medical intervention as the cornerstone principle of the company, ZCI's clinical staff is managed by a well-respected physician and nationally recognized occupational nurse. The medical staff remains accessible to workers, employers, and medical colleagues seeking information about a specific case. The ZCI clinical staff continually reaches out to participating companies with wellness programs, educational programs, and occupational health analyses to prevent injuries before they occur.

However, when an injury does occur, the ZCI staff continuously monitors the case from the moment of immediate clinical intervention, to its closure. By aggressively managing each individual case and providing detailed status and outcome reports to employers, ZCI lowers total costs associated with workers' compensation claims by 10 to 50 percent. The ZCI

At Span America Medical Systems Inc., ZCI Integrated Solutions Corp.'s manager of clinical affairs, Barbara Lassiter, R.N., conducts an on-site evaluation to prevent workplace injuries.

clinical affairs department monitors each case to ensure proper treatment protocol and case managers review each medical bill for accuracy, verifying that each approved bill only includes appropriate treatment, and is in compliance with the state fee schedule for workers' compensation claims.

"Businesses that incorporate a ZCI workers' compensation injury management plan not only provide the highest quality care to their injured workers, but also have significant improvements in their bottom line at the end of the year," West said. More importantly, with a personal, individualized approach, ZCI counsels individual workers and helps them return to a productive work environment as soon as medically appropriate. "We are responsive to both the employer and the employee's needs. Both need information and ultimately have the same goal—to recover and return to work," West said.

Through consultation with South Carolina businesses, ZCI allows companies to take a pro-active position in reducing workers' compensation claims and preventing injuries altogether. "The most serious mistake that businesses make is waiting until an accident occurs and then responding in a haphazard, inconsistent way. By establishing policies and relationships in advance, companies can make workers' compensation more manageable and less costly," Matula said.

Greenville Tech

*T*hirty-six years ago, Greenville Tech opened its doors on a piece of property that many people had judged unusable—the site of a former city dump. The college consisted of one building in which 800 students attended classes. Today, one building has grown to dozens, one campus has become a three-campus system, and the number of students has increased more than ten times over.

Greenville Tech was established in 1962 to ensure that Upstate businesses and industries would have a ready supply of well trained workers.

Just as Greenville Tech's growth has been strong and steady, the area the college supports has moved at a fast forward pace for some time. As the Upstate experiences phenomenal growth with a thriving economy and low unemployment, Greenville Tech is proud to have played a role in this process, serving as part of a team made up of educators, volunteers, government leaders, and members of the Chamber of Commerce working to drive economic development.

Today, Greenville is considered a prime location. Greenville County is making a name for itself far and wide and is now home to a sizable number of foreign-owned companies. Greenville's reputation as an excellent business location has drawn an impressive mix of American companies as well. When *Entrepreneur Magazine* selected the best cities in the country for small business recently, Greenville made the list, and Greenville Tech, with customized training programs for large and small businesses, was cited as one of the reasons.

Greenville Tech works closely with business and industry from the time a company first considers an Upstate location. South Carolina's Special Schools Program steps in where needed with intense pre-employment worker training that is modified and tailored to the specific needs of the company. Greenville Tech picks up where Special Schools leaves off, working with a company to determine its needs and to identify areas of training that will improve the organization. The college's role is to serve as a catalyst for the creation of jobs that broaden the county's tax base, not just by attracting business and industry, but by nurturing companies once they locate in the area. A recently-established Business and Industry Services department works closely with the business community, identifying training needs and developing solutions.

Just as companies benefit from the services that Greenville Tech provides, the college is fortunate to form connections with industry that enhance and enrich what the college offers. Each program has an advisory board made up of professionals from area businesses who make recommendations about what is taught and the resources needed to teach it. Once these resources have been determined, companies help Greenville Tech stretch equipment dollars by donating or lending current equipment so that students receive hands-on training that allows them to be assets in the workplace with little on-the-job training required.

Greenville Tech responds to industry and community needs by developing programs, schedules, and delivery modes that meet changing requirements. New programs are added as employment trends emerge. Students can choose the main campus, Greer Campus, or Brashier Campus. The college also offers teleclasses that are broadcast live from the main campus to remote locations, telecourses that can be viewed on cable television or on videocassette, and College Online which provides classes via computer.

Response to community needs was the reason the University Center was founded in 1987. In the eighties, business and

community leaders determined that the lack of a public four-year college or university within Greenville County was a deterrent to businesses considering the Upstate area. With the center, Greenville County has not one, but seven colleges and universities—all under one roof—in a building just down the street from Greenville Tech's main campus across from McAlister Square.

At the opposite end of the spectrum, community needs prompted the college to offer high school students a chance to get a head start on college through the Jump Start Program. This program sends Greenville Tech faculty into the high schools, where students take three-credit-hour courses for only $100. These courses transfer to practically any college or university the student should decide to attend, and they help to form a bridge from high school to college.

Responding to community needs means change—something that Greenville Tech has never shied away from. In fact, if there's a better way and the end result is improved customer service, the idea is studied, refined, and implemented. This kind of responsiveness has built the college into a national model and ensures that Greenville Tech will continue to be the "College That Works for Greenville." ◪

165

Greenville Tech takes great pride in its instructors. All are of the highest caliber, bringing real world experience to the classroom to better train students for the workforce.

HEALTHSOUTH

What began as a good idea for health-care delivery in 1984 is an even better idea today. Founded to improve patient outcomes while simultaneously reducing healthcare costs, HEALTHSOUTH is now the nation's largest provider of ambulatory surgery and outpatient rehabilitative healthcare and a leading provider of diagnostic imaging with more than 1,900 facilities in 50 states.

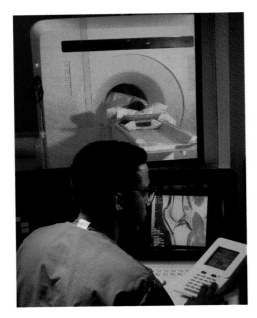

HEALTHSOUTH makes sure each of its facilities has the latest equipment and technology in order to deliver the most accurate results.

By combining ambulatory surgery and diagnostic imaging services with inpatient and outpatient rehabilitation through its Integrated Service Model, HEALTHSOUTH is able to emphasize value and consistent, quality care. The ISM allows patients to move through a seamless system of care with multiple points of entry so that patients can progress smoothly from one level of care to the next.

Diagnostics

A proper diagnosis ensures that the patient receives the correct treatment. That's why HEALTHSOUTH makes sure each of its diagnostic facilities has the latest equipment and technology. HEALTHSOUTH is committed to performing the most sophisticated tests and delivering the most accurate results. This guarantees that patients receive the highest quality care and physicians receive accurate, reliable results on every patient they refer. Diagnostic services include: MRI, MRA, CT, nuclear medicine, ultrasound, mammography, bone density, cardiology, fluoroscopy, and x-ray.

Surgery

HEALTHSOUTH is the nation's largest provider of outpatient surgical services. Each surgical facility offers the safest, highest quality surgical care. HEALTH-SOUTH's facilities are specifically designed and staffed for surgical procedures that can be performed on a same-day basis. Each facility is comfortable and fully accredited. Surgery services include ENT, general surgery, gynecology, oral surgery, orthopaedics, pain management, plastic surgery, podiatry, and urology.

Rehabilitation

HEALTHSOUTH is the nation's largest provider of sports medicine and outpatient rehabilitation. At each facility, skilled therapists and trainers provide the highest quality and most cost-effective care available. HEALTHSOUTH has earned a national reputation for producing results by achieving and documenting excellent outcomes for their patients. Rehabilitation services include: arthritis; back stabilization; foot care; functional capacity evaluation; lymphedema; orthopaedic; orthotics; pain management; spinal disorders; TMJ; work hardening; wound care, including acute and chronic burn care; and edema, including venous, traumatic, and post-op.

HEALTHSOUTH's impact on the Upstate extends beyond the rehabilitation setting. HEALTHSOUTH is a prominent supporter of many service organizations, including the American Heart Association, the Arthritis Foundation, United Cerebral Palsy, and the American Cancer Society. In addition, HEALTHSOUTH employees are leaders in numerous civic and philanthropic organizations in the Upstate region.

Perhaps, though, HEALTHSOUTH's role is best demonstrated by the success stories of its patients—a teenager who has triumphed over a coma or a stroke victim who is speaking again. Restoring independence is a daily endeavor and achievement at HEALTHSOUTH.

To ensure that patients, as well as the general public, remain informed about the facility, HEALTHSOUTH maintains a website at www.healthsouth.com. This website may be used to locate the nearest facility or to attain general information about HEALTHSOUTH.

HEALTHSOUTH is dedicated to providing expert, cost-effective care, producing excellent outcome, and getting people back . . . to work . . . to play . . . to living. ☺

HEALTHSOUTH has attracted some of the biggest names in sports including Michael Jordan, Mary Joe Fernandez, and, pictured below, Bo Jackson.

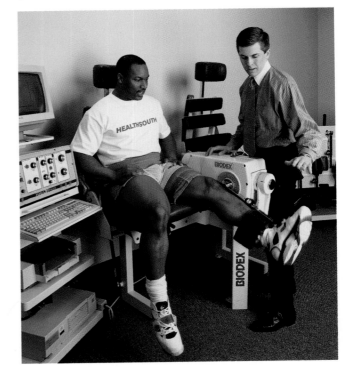

14

Chapter Fourteen

Marketplace

Hyatt Regency Greenville

Since opening its doors in January of 1982, the Hyatt Regency Greenville has taken pride in being "Greenville's Hotel." The prestigious distinction came in part due to the hotel serving as the nucleus for the revitalization of the city's Central Business and Entertainment District.

In the late 1960s and early 1970s, downtown Greenville began to experience deterioration as a result of residents moving to surrounding communities to make their homes, and retail stores choosing mall settings as opposed to downtown streets.

In 1975, after many failed revitalization attempts, the mayor of Greenville initiated a major effort to combine private and public investment to undertake a series of projects in downtown. The city hired a consultant to assist in the development of alternatives for revitalizing downtown Greenville. At that time, a hotel, convention center, and public commons complex were determined to be the key ingredients in a larger program of additional downtown improvements.

In early 1977, the Hyatt Corporation entered into a partnership with the City of

The Hyatt Regency Greenville has established itself as being a citywide attraction as well as serving as the Northern anchor of Main Street.

Greenville and the Greenville Community Corporation to develop Greenville Commons, which now houses the Hyatt Regency, a convention center and an office complex. To make Greenville Commons a reality, the Hyatt Corporation agreed to make $3 million available as its share of the partnership, and the Greenville Community Corporation—comprised of approximately 30 local individuals and companies—agreed to make $5 million available. In order to complete the private financing, a $16 million loan was secured.

Public financing was provided in the sum of $10 million by the City of Greenville. The city's share consisted of a $5.5 million urban development action grant, a second grant of approximately $2 million from the Economic Development Administration and $2.5 million from the city's general fund reserve.

A groundbreaking for the $34-million project was held in January of 1979. The office building and parking garage were completed in 1980. The Hyatt Regency and convention center opened in January of 1982.

A significant result of the Hyatt's opening along with the Greenville Commons complex were the vast improvements that were made to the surrounding area. Traffic lanes on Main Street were reduced from

four to two lanes, and cosmetic and safety measures such as wider sidewalks, plantings, street furniture, mid-block pedestrian crosswalks, and vehicular and pedestrian lighting systems were added.

Through the years, the Hyatt Regency Greenville has established itself as a citywide attraction as well as serving as the northern anchor of Main Street. "We view ourselves as the catalyst behind the restoration of downtown Greenville," said Pat Trammell, director of sales for Hyatt.

The Hyatt Regency Greenville is conveniently located in the Central Business and Entertainment District at 220 North Main Street. The 330-room convention hotel, including 18 suites, is within walking distance of the Museum of Art, Peace Center for the Performing Arts, the BI-LO Center, as well as downtown restaurants and shops. The Hyatt is within five miles of the Palmetto International Exposition Center and only 14 miles from the Greenville-Spartanburg International Airport, where complimentary shuttle service is available to and from the Hyatt.

The hotel, convention center, and atrium are managed by Hyatt Hotels under a management agreement with Hyatt Greenville. Although the atrium functions as a major portion of the hotel lobby, it has remained public space. The management agreement with Hyatt Greenville also stipulates that while the convention center is operated by Hyatt Hotels, it must retain its public character by being accessible to all groups and individuals who desire to conduct meetings in the facility.

The Hyatt Regency Greenville is settled within the lush, eight-story atrium lobby featuring a cascading waterfall, extensive landscaping, fountains and brooks, making for a magnificent introduction to this remarkable hotel.

Even more special than the facility is the way the friendly staff caters to the guests with a touch of Southern hospitality. The Hyatt Regency makes sure each guest's stay is as comfortable and productive as possible. The specially designed Hyatt Business Plan accommodations are equipped with a comfortable work station,

The convention center, which is operated by Hyatt Hotels, is accessible to all groups and individuals who desire to conduct meetings in the facility.

fax machine, personal amenities, plus a printer and copier.

"A large percentage of our guests are usually in town on business, therefore we make sure they have all the conveniences they need to make their stay as productive as possible," Trammell said.

The hotel offers convenient parking for all its guests in the form of an adjacent parking garage. As another added convenience, The Hyatt Regency boasts being the first hotel in Greenville to offer a full-service valet parking for its guests.

First-class dining is available at the Provencia Restaurant, located in the atrium. The restaurant offers succulent Italian cuisine with a Mediterranean twist. The Commons Bar, also located in the atrium, offers guests the opportunity to enjoy exotic beverages served in an inviting atmosphere.

Hyatt Regency also provides a fully equipped exercise facility. Guests who enjoy working up a sweat can stay with

their regular workout routine. A whirlpool and outdoor pool is available for those guests who just want to relax. Activities such as golf, tennis, hiking, fishing, and whitewater rafting in the Blue Ridge Mountains are nearby.

Trammell said along with being "Greenville's Hotel" comes a great deal of responsibility. Hyatt is very serious about the appearance of its facilities and the satisfaction of its guests. "We have owners who are committed to the quality of the product, from the facilities to the services and amenities we offer our guests," Trammell said.

The ownership of Hyatt is also adamant about staying involved in the community. "The hotel's mission is to continue as an active corporate citizen," Trammell said. "We encourage everyone from our general managers to our front-line employees to participate in charitable and civic organizations," she said.

But Hyatt's participation in the community doesn't stop there. "Hyatt backs the efforts of its employees with contributions and support services," Trammell said, further indicating how the Hyatt Regency has grown to become the heartbeat of a vibrant and vital downtown Greenville. The Hyatt Regency's purpose in Greenville far exceeds the role that most companies play within their communities. These days, as visitors stroll through the bustling downtown streets, they can regard the Hyatt Regency as a Greenville mainstay, forever intertwined with the destiny of the city. 🔳

171

The eight-story atrium lobby featuring magnificent landscaping, lush greenery, cascading waterfalls, and fountains makes for a magnificent introduction to this remarkable hotel.

BI-LO

"**O**ur marketing strategy is based entirely on people: associates, customers, and the community. That's what sets us apart from the competition," according to Marsh Collins, president and CEO of BI-LO, Inc. The commitment to be the preferred supermarket in each community BI-LO serves is also what makes the Mauldin-based company one of the most progressive and rapidly growing supermarket chains in the southeastern United States.

The Southeast has the highest supermarket growth in the United States, and BI-LO is a significant part of that growth. According to Collins, low profit margins are the norm in the supermarket industry, and supermarkets must depend on volume sales and steady growth to increase market share.

BI-LO's roots are in the Upstate, beginning operation in 1961 with four stores and soon recognized for quality products, low prices, and the familiar BI-LO bull displayed on top of each store. Today, BI-LO operates over 260 stores in the Carolinas, Georgia, and Tennessee. It is one of the largest employers in Greenville County and in South Carolina, with a total company-wide employment of over 25,000 and annual sales approaching $3 billion.

In such a competitive business, success is no accident. Each year BI-LO invests heavily in its most valuable assets: the communities it serves and the supermarket facilities it operates. With careful, planned capital expenditures on new stores and expansion of existing supermarkets, BI-LO pledges to continue the steady growth it has enjoyed over the past three and a half decades.

One marketing initiative that has paid substantial dividends to BI-LO's strategy of customer satisfaction has been the development and implementation of the BI-LO BONUSCARD. The BONUSCARD allows BI-LO customers to take advantage of outstanding prices on groceries while offering extra rewards for loyal customers. BI-LO shoppers have enjoyed special discounts and exciting sweepstakes offers using their BONUSCARDS. The company's successful card-based reward program has become the standard in the grocery industry for its innovation and customer approval.

An essential element of today's supermarket experience is to make grocery shopping as pleasant and convenient as possible. Many BI-LO stores feature floral and seafood shops, pharmacies, expanded international food and wine departments, as well as enlarged, service-oriented delicatessens and bakeries. BI-LO believes that the future of the supermarket industry lies in the diversity of the facility.

Convenience is what counts at BI-LO stores. "If we can add more services and still maintain our own identity, we will do

Marsh Collins, President and CEO of BI-LO.

it. It depends on the preferences of our customers," says Collins. "Neighborhood marketing is possible now, and we intend to provide the customers in each neighborhood with the products and services they desire. Simply put, that is the cornerstone of BI-LO's continued success."

And BI-LO strengthens that commitment through the growth and promotion of its associates. Career planning for associates, along with the training and education needed to offer superior customer satisfaction at BI-LO, is fundamental to the business philosophy. Opportunities for career advancement and growth are available at all levels of the business. BI-LO

creates a work environment that protects the dignity of each associate and guarantees fair and equitable compensation. BI-LO also believes that there is always room for innovation and encourages input from its associates.

Although BI-LO is a familiar name in South Carolina, Royal Ahold is not. BI-LO's parent company since 1977, Royal Ahold is an international retail organization with headquarters in the Netherlands. Royal Ahold owns grocery chains on four continents, including Europe, North America, and South America, representing more than 3,200 stores and 220,000 associates world-wide. Ahold stock is traded on the New York Stock Exchange.

BI-LO was Royal Ahold's first major acquisition in North America. Other Ahold USA companies include Giant Food Stores (Carlisle, PA), Stop & Shop (Boston, MA), and Tops Markets (Buffalo, NY).

Being part of a worldwide organization has not stopped BI-LO from being a part of their local communities. BI-LO is committed to being a good corporate citizen by participating in many charitable events

and supporting countless nonprofit organizations. The list of organizations receiving assistance is too long to mention in its entirety, but includes the YMCA, YWCA, Meals on Wheels, Urban League of the Upstate, March of Dimes, Junior Achievement, Special Olympics, Governors School for the Arts, Boy Scouts, and Girl Scouts. BI-LO is a pacesetter company for the United Way campaign, assisting hundreds of agencies that provide services to our neighbors in need. All of these groups are wholeheartedly supported by BI-LO both with funding and with

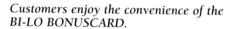
Customers enjoy the convenience of the BI-LO BONUSCARD.

173

volunteer hours given generously by its associates.

BI-LO is also responsible for helping to make the BI-LO Center in downtown Greenville a reality. The 16,000 seat sports and entertainment complex adds a new dimension to entertainment opportunities in the Upstate as it hosts a wide array of community and family events. The BI-LO Center will be home to the Greenville Grrrowl East Coast Hockey League team.

"We have been blessed with success, and giving back to our communities is one way we can say thank you," says Collins.

Commitment to customer satisfaction, innovation, convenience, and low prices—it's all part of building a better business. In Greenville, it's all part of building a better BI-LO.

Palmetto Expo Center

Long known as Textile Hall and the home of the American Textile Machinery Exhibition-International, Greenville's Palmetto Expo Center today hosts more than 500 events annually from smaller corporate meetings to international trade shows.

Textile Hall was renamed Palmetto Expo Center in 1986 and was given a $4 million facelift that included air conditioning the facility's four exhibit halls, and lighting and landscaping the 17 acres of parking areas surrounding the building. But the transformation began in earnest in 1993 with the opening of the 88,000 square-foot James H. Woodside Conference Center—a move that elevated Palmetto Expo Center to convention center status and made it a formidable competitor in the meetings and trade show industry nationwide.

Privately owned by the Greenville, South Carolina based Textile Hall Corporation, Palmetto Expo Center receives no public funding for its operations or capital improvements. The facility opened in 1964 off South Carolina Highway 291 next to Greenville's Downtown Airport with 120,000 square-feet of exhibit space. A growing American Textile Machinery Exhibition-International dictated four building expansions and by 1977, Greenville's exhibit facility was among the largest in the Southeast with 375,000 square-feet of space.

Founded in 1915 as a show management company to produce expositions primarily for the textile industry, Textile Hall Corporation today produces two consumer and four trade shows, all of which are held at Palmetto Expo Center. The American Textile Machinery Exhibition-International remains the Expo Center's largest show, drawing exhibitors and attendees from 45 states and more than 60 other countries to Greenville every three years. Other shows produced by Textile Hall Corporation are the Fiber Producer Exhibition & Conference; Textile Industries Supplies & Services Exhibition & Conference; Workplace Business to Business Conference & Expo; Holiday Fair; and the Boat, RV & Sports Show.

Palmetto Expo Center features four exhibition halls totalling 375,000 square-feet, 18 meeting rooms totaling more than 35,000 square-feet, an outdoor courtyard, more than 8,000 square-feet of prefunction space, and parking for 2,500 vehicles. The Woodside Conference Center also houses a 6,000 square-foot banquet kitchen giving Palmetto Expo Center Catering Services the ability to provide on-site, full-service catering and concessions.

Other in-house services include audio-visual, decorating, electrical, plumbing, teleconferencing, and telecommunications.

"There is no question that the addition of the Woodside Conference Center has given us the ability to compete for corporate meetings, association business, and citywide conventions," said Butler Mullins, president of Palmetto Expo Center, Inc. "We realized a dramatic increase in

The 1997 edition of the American Textile Machinery Exhibition-International (ATME-I). The largest show of its kind in the Western Hemisphere.

bookings the first year, and we continue to expand our markets."

In 1993, there were 170 events held at Palmetto Expo Center with a total attendance of 206,016. In 1994, with the first full year of operation of the Woodside Conference Center, the number of events more than doubled, reaching 368, and the number of visitors rose to 261,591. And in 1997, the center held 460 events with attendance totalling 344,576.

Location and Greenville business help sell Palmetto Expo Center

Because of its central location in the city of Greenville and Greenville's geographic desirability along Interstate 85, halfway between Atlanta and Charlotte, Palmetto Expo Center is a natural venue for show producers and meeting planners seeking a Southeastern audience. Located in the foothills of the majestic Blue Ridge Mountains, Greenville lies in South Carolina's northwest corner at the center of the state's most populous and prosperous region—the Upstate.

With a market area population of more than one million, Greenville ranks number one in retail sales in South Carolina and is part of the 35th largest television market in the United States.

Long recognized as the Textile Capital of the World, Greenville today boasts a diverse economy, a multicultural population, and a well-deserved reputation as a center for higher education and the arts.

The same ingredients that have made Greenville successful in luring manufacturing facilities and regional and corporate headquarters to the area are helping build the city's meetings and convention industry.

With more than 2,200 manufacturing facilities in the Upstate region of South Carolina, Greenville and the Palmetto Expo Center can deliver a solid exhibitor and attendee base for many types of manufacturing and industrial trade shows. Greenville also ranks as one of the four engineering centers in the world and has more engineers per capita than any other county in the United States. The area's economic base includes a healthy mix of growth industries including automotive, chemicals, plastics, transportation, rubber, and electronics.

Leisure activities enhance Greenville's convention industry

During leisure hours, Greenville residents play as hard as they work. The Greenville area offers 30 semi-private and public golf courses; water sports on Lakes Hartwell, Keowee, and Jocassee; and white water rafting along the scenic Nantahala and Chatooga Rivers. Moreover, galleries at Bob Jones University feature the largest collection of religious art in the world. So, whether leisure time is consumed by playing hard or spending some quiet time enjoying the arts, the Greenville area has much to offer.

175

Alpha Kappa Alpha Sorority 1997 South Atlantic Regional Conference.

Embassy Suites Golf Resort and Conference Center

A t the heart of Greenville's hottest growth area stands Embassy Suites Golf Resort and Conference Center, which has become a favorite destination of business travelers and golf enthusiasts alike.

The Embassy Suites Golf Resort and Conference Center, one of Greenville's premiere hotels, featuring deluxe accommodations, four lighted tennis courts, 20,000 square-feet of meeting space, and much more, is conveniently located just off I-85 near the I-385 interchange.

Located adjacent to the spectacular Verdae Greens Golf Course, Embassy Suites Golf Resort and Conference Center is the only golf resort and conference center in Greenville. "The golf course certainly makes us a favorite meeting facility for business travelers and companies when they're in Greenville," states General Manager Patrick Wilson. "Many companies build golf outings into their agendas and that has been very successful for them, and for us as well."

The nine-story, 268-suite hotel is operated by John Q. Hammons Hotels, Inc., a public company traded on the New York Stock Exchange. Hammons Hotels owns and operates more than 50 hotels nationwide. The local hotel is also part of the Embassy Suites family of more than 140 hotels worldwide.

The Greenville Embassy Suites opened in April 1993 and is located at 670 Verdae Boulevard just off I-85 near the I-385 interchange. Its convenient location is within minutes of the Greenville-Spartanburg International Airport, downtown, and such attractions as the Palmetto Expo

Center, Greenville Zoo, the Roper Mountain Science Center, the Greenville County Museum of Art, and the Reedy River Falls Historic Park.

As one of Greenville's premiere hotels, the Embassy Suites features deluxe accommodations, a championship golf course, four lighted tennis courts, 20,000 square-feet of meeting space, a scenic atrium, a full-service restaurant, lounge, fitness area, and much more.

The Embassy Suites offers a variety of accommodations to visitors. The spacious and comfortable two-room suites which include two telephones, two remote control TVs, coffee maker, refrigerator, microwave oven, and wet bar make for an enjoyable stay whether its business or pleasure. Also offered is the Presidential Suite which includes two TVs, two phones, living room, wet bar, a spacious king bedroom with separate dressing area, and an oversized whirlpool tub. Each guest also enjoys complimentary beverages at a manager's reception every evening, plus a cooked-to-order breakfast each morning along with a complimentary daily newspaper.

Championship greens and fairways are as close as exiting the main entrance of the Greenville Embassy Suites. Verdae Greens Golf Club is located adjacent to the hotel. This 18 hole, par 72 championship golf course, designed by Willard C. Byrd, was carved into a lush Carolina forest with hills and mountain-like brooks, making Verdae both scenic and challenging to play.

Verdae Greens offers a fully equipped golf

shop with the most recent golf fashions, a full service bar and grill, a large driving range and putting green, Pencross Bentgrass greens and Bermuda tees and fairways.

The club welcomes corporate and private golf outings, offering specialty golf clinics, food and beverage catering before, during, and after the clinics, and an outdoor party deck for social gatherings. Private golf instruction from PGA professionals, overnight club regripping, and available rental clubs are just a few of the extras offered at Verdae Greens Golf Club. Golf memberships are also available.

In conjunction with the golf club, the

Located adjacent to the Embassy Suites Golf Resort and Conference Center is the spectacular Verdae Greens Golf Course. This championship course offers a challenging game while displaying a scenic view of the Carolina forest.

Embassy Suites co-sponsors the PGA Tour Nike Upstate Classic, an annual golf tournament which benefits a number of local charities. Throughout the years, the hotel and golf club have supported the Boys & Girls Club, the Greenville Chapter of the Salvation Army, and the Ronald McDonald House.

Whether it's a business meeting or a wedding reception, Embassy Suites is proud to be of service with more than 20,000 square-feet of convention space, which is divisible into a wide variety of room configurations. Exclusive banquet facilities seat up to 1,000 and an outdoor entertainment deck comfortably serves an additional 500 guests. A complete array of audio-visual, public address, and lighting systems round out the finest meeting place in the Upstate.

Staying in shape is easy at Embassy Suites. The fully-equipped fitness center which includes state-of-the-art exercycles, treadmills, rowing machines, and more are available for guests to sharpen their senses and work out their tensions. Or for a more leisurely experience, guests can stretch out on the sun deck, relax in the whirlpool or sauna, or dive into one of the pools—indoors or out.

The hotel also offers convenient food

Whether visiting for business or pleasure, the comfortable and spacious two-room suites offered at the Embassy Suites include all of the amenities to make the guests' stay as enjoyable as possible.

and beverage options. The 19th Green is the perfect place to relax and unwind with a favorite beverage, meet friends, and listen to the soothing sounds of rippling pools and fountains, all set in a beautiful garden atrium. For an unmatched dining experience in a casual, relaxing atmosphere, try Cafe Verdae. Features include a private dining area for parties up to thirty, which can be reserved for special occasions.

The hotel's prominence in Greenville is based on far more than its beautiful facilities and championship golf course. Award-winning services and first-class amenities figure strongly into the hotel's reputation for excellence. The hotel is consistently among the top five Embassy Suites in the world for total quality index. Criteria for the prestigious "Rose Award" is based on guest feedback on overall customer satisfaction, the fewest number of guest complaints, and how complaints are handled when they are received. The hotel ranked as the number one Embassy Suites in the world for this distinction in 1995 and again in 1997.

In addition, Cafe Verdae has been ranked a top five restaurant in the Embassy Suites hotel system. Criteria for this award includes atmosphere, cleanliness, food quality and taste, value, service, and performance.

"Maintaining our consistently high level of excellence in quality and service is due primarily to the hard work and dedication

Upon entering the Embassy Suites, any guest can't help but notice the beautiful atrium designed with a maze of walkways surrounded by lush greenery, blooming flowers, a flowing brook, and soft lights.

of our staff members, who are most deserving of these awards," Wilson said.

Whether it's picking up a guest at the airport on time or a friendly smile from an employee welcoming a guest to town, the staff at Embassy Suites works hard every day to create a hospitable atmosphere. This ensures each guest feels good about their visit to the hotel and Greenville, and will want to visit again, very soon.

Stax's Restaurants

George Stathakis, co-owner of Stax's Restaurants, entered the restaurant business in 1975 when he purchased a luncheonette on Poinsett Highway featuring Southern style, down-home meals. That restaurant—Stax's Original—was just the beginning in a fine tradition of dining in Greenville.

Today, six restaurants, a catering service, a bakery, and a piano bar carry the Stax name. "Greenville's success has been our success," says Stathakis. Future expansion isn't out of the question at this point, but growth will remain within the family of the ownership. "We'll never become a chain," says Stathakis, "because we'll always have personal attention at our restaurants. We'll always have a person with ownership in the restaurants at each location—or there won't be a restaurant."

As Greenville has experienced rapid economic development and growth during the past 20 years, Stathakis has experienced success of his own as well. With typical entrepreneurial foresight, Stathakis saw a niche for an upscale fine-dining restaurant in the city. So in 1986, he opened Stax's Peppermill, hiring Stanley Coumos, a talented chef from Chicago, to run the kitchen. The following year,

Stax's International Bakery, occupied by 5,000-square-feet of world-class breads and pastries, provide all of Stax's restaurants with a wide variety of delicious baked goods.

Coumos became a business partner and remains an owner and close friend of Stathakis' today.

Stax's Peppermill was an immediate success. It has been voted "Best Restaurant in Greenville" more than once and has won countless local awards and several national awards. Currently, it is listed among the top 200 restaurants in the nation by numerous trade publications.

One reason that customers keep coming back to Stax's Peppermill is the beef.

"We make a very big issue out of purchasing beef," Stathakis says. "It's not easy to do, and it is rarely done the way we do it." He says the Peppermill is the only restaurant in Greenville that serves certified 'prime' beef, which includes only one percent of all beef in the world.

"The steak doesn't cost the customer much more, but if paying $15 versus $17, why not get the Cadillac of beef?" Stathakis says. "We commit to the best no matter what the cost."

Located next to the Peppermill is the Stax's Piano Bar, which offers live entertainment Tuesday through Saturday evenings, headlining pianist/vocalist Dwight Woods and a variety of auxiliary talent.

After experiencing such success with the Peppermill, Stathakis and Coumos began looking for additional opportunities for growth and expansion. In 1988, the partners opened Stax's Omega, a diner-type establishment known for its all day breakfasts. A year later, they acquired 5,000-square-feet of property next door, and opened Stax's International Bakery, specializing in Greek, French, Italian, and

Whether a lunch crowd or an evening dinner, Stax's Grill provides only top quality dining to its customers.

other world-class breads and pastries. "The reason for adding the bakery was so we would have fresh breads and desserts for the restaurants, maintain a retail outlet for these goods, as well as offer catering services," Stathakis says.

The Omega and the Bakery proved so successful, the Stax's group purchased the shopping center in which the two businesses are located. As a complement to that growth, in 1990, Stax's Grill was opened, featuring Sterling Silver beef, the second highest quality of beef. Between the Peppermill and the Grill, only the top five percent of beef quality is put before customers. To operate the Grill, Stathakis brought in cousin Charlie Cavalaris, now a third partner. Cavalaris was formerly a top sales representative with foodservice supplier PYA/Monarch, with whom Stax's did—and still does—a great deal of business with.

Since it opened in 1986, Stax Peppermill has remained a successful fine-dining restaurant receiving countless awards. Currently, it is listed among the top 200 restaurants in the nation by numerous trade publications.

Last, but not least, Stax's newest enterprise—Carolina Roasters—operates in the Haywood Mall Food Court.

Carolina Roasters is playing an important role in the growth of the Stax's catering business which serves corporate as well as private customers. Catering Director Jean French-Turner oversees this particular operation.

Stax's doesn't compromise quality by serving frozen food in any of the their restaurants. They only accept top quality produce from their vendors. Stathakis and Coumos make it a point to know all of their vendors personally. They travel around the world and across the country to get the best food and furnishings for the restaurants. "It's nothing for one of us to get on a plane and go to Chicago, the Gulf Coast, or Miami," Stathakis says. "Of course, we don't recoup the cost of buying lobster tails that way, but we get the best—and if we can't get the best, we don't sell it."

Corporate Community

The corporate community is a large portion of Stax's customer base, and as an incentive to those customers, the Corporate Club was established to offer special perks to frequent diners.

The club, which is 1,500 members strong, is a program where businesses, based on how much entertaining their company does, receives a package of discounts and incentives at the Stax's restaurants. "Stax's gets repeat business, and the corporate customer gets about a 20 percent discount while impressing their clients. It's like having a private caterer," Stathakis says.

Perks of the Corporate Club include no membership dues, monthly billing with no service charge, discounts on food and beverages, personalized menus, and a complimentary cocktail reception with some events.

Primarily utilizing the Peppermill, there are private rooms that can be reserved for a few hours or an entire day. These rooms accommodate meetings of six to 150 persons and visual aid equipment is accessible if needed.

"Why not eat at the nicest restaurant in Greenville for comparable prices to other restaurants and hotels," Stathakis says.

Interest in the Corporate Club has been so brisk, that reservations are being made six months in advance and a long list of clients are waiting to join.

Employees: The Key To Succes

Much of the success Stax's Restaurants has experienced throughout the years can be credited to skilled and loyal employees. "You've got to hire good people, the right people," Stathakis says. "Treat them right, pay them well, and they will make you successful."

Stax's makes it a point to hire professionals who are serious about the restaurant business, and the company wants them to succeed.

"We want all of our employees to do well," Stathakis says. "Their success is our success and vice versa." "Without our employees, Stax's wouldn't be Stax's," he says. ◗

In 1988, a diner-type establishment named Stax's Omega, was opened and has since become known for its all day breakfasts.

Hilton Greenville and Towers

L ocated at 45 West Orchard Park Drive just off of Haywood Road and I-385 in Greenville's vibrant Eastside, the Hilton Greenville and Towers is situated in an ideal suburban setting, and is convenient to all business and entertainment activities, downtown, and the Greenville-Spartanburg International Airport. The Hilton is also Greenville's closest full-service hotel to the Palmetto Expo Center.

Designed to fulfill every need of today's business and leisure traveler, the Hilton's extraordinary attention to detail and Southern ambiance greets guests at every turn. The professional and gracious staff offers guests nothing but the very best services available anywhere.

"Our guests and customers deserve the best and it's our goal to make sure every

With 256 guestrooms, including six suites, and over 12,000 square feet of flexible meeting space, the Hilton Greenville and Towers is one of the city's premiere full-service hotels.

customer is 100 percent satisfied with our services, and if they're not, then we want them to let us know," said Bill Bennett, director of sales and marketing for the local Hilton.

The Hilton's commitment to its guests hasn't gone unnoticed. For the past three years, the Hilton Greenville and Towers has been ranked in the top four among 48 Hilton Hotels across the Southeast for its superior customer satisfaction marks.

The 256-guest room hotel, which includes six suites, opened in 1987. The hotel is owned and operated by the Peabody Hotel Group, which is famous for the world-famous Peabody Ducks.

All guest rooms are spacious and include smart desks, two 2-line telephones with data ports, irons and ironing boards, hair dryers, and coffee makers. Guests may also choose to stay on the exclusive Towers floor, which offers an array of personalized services including private key access, concierge services, upgraded guest room amenities, and access to a private lounge offering complimentary continental breakfast, evening hors d'oeuvres, and an honor bar.

Guest's who may require the necessities of an office during their stay may choose to utilize the Hilton's Executive Business Center which features personal computers and printers, a copier and fax machine, modem hook-ups, and secretarial support.

The hotel also features The Marketplace Restaurant which offers exceptional cuisine along with Southern hospitality.

A health club featuring treadmills, stairclimbers, rowers, sauna, and whirlpool is available for guests who desire a light to moderate workout. For more ambitious guests, a more strenuous

The beautifully decorated lobby serves as a grand entrance to the Hilton Greenville and Towers.

workout is available through Hilton's complimentary access to nearby Gold's Gym. The hotel also boasts a retractable roof making for an indoor/outdoor pool so guests may enjoy a swim, no matter what the season.

Additional services provided by the Hilton include complimentary airport transportation, complimentary parking, room service, same day laundry, and valet service. Hilton also has arrangements with Cross Winds, a nearby par three golf course, and Willow Creek Golf Course for golf enthusiasts.

A professional catering and banquet staff hosts business meetings and wedding receptions on a regular basis in the Hilton's 12,000 square feet of flexible meeting space. The top-quality staff works closely with local vendors such as florists, decorators, and entertainment companies to make sure all events are a great success.

The Hilton Greenville and Towers prides itself on offering the best services guests may require. Whether staying for business purposes or pleasure, accommodations are always above expectations.

Seven Oaks and Restaurant YAGOTO

With the Wisteria in full bloom, spring arrives with the toss of a bridal bouquet. Enjoy live jazz on the veranda as a gentle breeze cools the lazy days of summer. When the days fall shorter, and the nights cooler, the colorful trees beckon you to sit a while longer. In the winter, with the fireplaces lit, the house is aglow with friends and festivities. For years, Seven Oaks has been celebrating the seasons in Greenville.

Built in 1895, Seven Oaks is a nostalgic reminder of days gone by. This Victorian mansion located downtown in the Pettigru Historic District is surrounded by old oaks and flowering gardens. Inside the house, the original design has been maintained. The fireplaces, stained glass windows, and the mosaic foyer are just a few images of the living past.

But there is a twist . . . and it's Southern! There is nothing old-fashioned about Chef Liz Minetta's innovative cuisine. Try the shrimp and lobster cake, the "eggroll" stuffed quail, or her marinated veal strip steak. Chef Liz's talents never cease to amaze! And don't forget the Seven Oaks' signature Belgian Chocolate Chip Cookie served hot from the oven. Heavenly decadence!

Seven Oaks features creative American cuisine with a new South twist. Seven Oaks is available for corporate parties, wedding receptions, and other social gatherings.

Restaurant YAGOTO

"Behind the wall, behind the mall" Restaurant YAGOTO introduced Japanese cuisine to Greenville. Beyond a mere stone hedge visitors may stroll in the Japanese gardens with a quiet stream, lotus blossoms, and a visiting crane. The building is fourteenth century Japanese architecture, historically home to shogun warlords. Each dining room offers a different view of the enclosed rock garden which was modeled after the famous *Ryoan-ji*.

Dining guests select their own experience—enjoy shoeless comfort in the tatami rooms, practice Japanese with the sushi chef at the sushi bar (and let him practice his English as well), or admire the ikebana arrangement while seated at a traditional dining table. There is something for everyone.

For over 10 years, Restaurant YAGOTO has set the standard for other Japanese restaurants to follow. Chef Fukuhara is an acknowledged "guru" of Japanese cooking.

Seven Oaks Restaurant, located at 104 Broadus Avenue in Greenville, serves Southern cuisine and is open Monday through Saturday for dinner and available for private or corporate gatherings.

His presentations and daily specials have secured his reputation as the leader of his field. The menu offers a comprehensive selection: sushi, sukiyaki, shabu-shabu, tempura, teppanyaki, and teriyaki dishes just to name a few. Or, do as the Japanese do, say "omakase" and leave it up to Chef Fukuhara.

Restaurant YAGOTO is open for dinner and is available for luncheons, corporate gatherings, and other social events.

The Nippon Center

Restaurant YAGOTO is located within the Nippon Center. A Japanese cultural center, the Center promotes cultural exchange with classes, demonstrations, and festivals held throughout the year. The Center is available to the public for tours and school field trips. ◩

Restaurant YAGOTO, located at 500 Congaree Road, Greenville, in The Nippon Center, is surrounded by lush strolling gardens. Each dining room offers a view of the enclosed rock garden modeled after **Ryoan-ji** *in Kyoto, Japan.*

181

S.B. Phillips Company, Inc.

People. They are the heart and soul of business. Forget assets, core competencies, competitive advantages—the effective management of people resources can mean the success or failure of a company.

In addition to Phillips' corporate headquarters in Greenville (pictured), the company has grown to over 25 offices throughout the Southeast in North and South Carolina, Tennessee, Virginia, and Alabama.

182

Since 1968, S.B. Phillips Company, Inc. has been helping companies throughout Greenville and the Southeast manage these all-important resources. Blending all facets of human resource management, from temporary and facility staffing to permanent placement and outplacement, the divisions of Phillips have forged strong relationships and proven themselves reliable and committed partners to their client companies for over thirty years.

Sam B. Phillips, Jr. founded the company in May 1968. At that time, he was a pioneer in contract labor and recruiting, focusing primarily on the region's thriving textile industry. Growing rapidly into a wider range of services, the company expanded into search and placement as well as temporary staffing.

Today, S.B. Phillips Company employs over 200 full-time employees and thousands of contract and temporary workers in over 25 offices throughout the Southeast. During the extensive growth, the company's strong suit continues to be its hands-on, focused approach to people—both employees and clients.

"We see the employee, the individual person, as the critical aspect of every relationship we have," says Phillips. "Finding, attracting, and retaining the best people is our principal goal. By doing that, we can take away our clients' personnel worries and allow them to concentrate on making and selling their products and services."

"In other words," he continues, "we do what *we* do best so that they can do what *they* do best."

To that end, Phillips has always offered the very best in benefits and services to its employees. The employee package includes insurance, vacation days, holiday pay, a 401(k) profit sharing plan, training and life enrichment programs, as well as many other valuable opportunities.

S.B. Phillips Company is comprised of four core groups. *Phillips Staffing's* range of services includes clerical, customer service, and light industrial personnel in every capacity, from short-term and vacancy fill-in to long-term and facility staffing. *Phillips Technical Staffing* provides contract labor services for continuous maintenance, modification, outage support, and other functions to the power, pulp and paper, textile, aircraft, and a wide variety of manufacturing industries nationwide. *Phillips Resource Group* supports clients through executive search, recruiting and placement of talented professionals, as well as outplacement services. And *Phillips Technology Consulting* offers a variety of computer contract labor services to assist clients in meeting their information technology challenges.

In 1998, Phillips expanded to include a professional employment organization (PEO) to serve the needs of many other companies, both small and large. The talented, experienced staff lends its expertise to provide full-scale personnel outsourcing through this newest division.

The company also owns PhilChem,

Inc., a subsidiary that manufactures and distributes several lines of specialty chemicals used to manufacture pulp, paper, and textile products. From its state-of-the-art, zero emissions chemical plant in Greer, PhilChem provides top-notch technology and services to its clients worldwide.

S.B. Phillips Company's involvement extends beyond the business arena as well. The company encourages its employees to participate in civic activities and events. Sam Phillips leads by example in Greenville—he was instrumental in building Greenville Municipal Stadium and bringing the Braves AA professional baseball team to town, and he has participated in numerous other efforts locally including the Timmons Arena at Furman University.

S.B. Phillips Company founder and owner, Sam B. Phillips, Jr. (right) and vice president S. Blanton Phillips, III (left).

Continual innovation in the human resources field, unceasing client support, and most importantly, attention to people have made S.B. Phillips Company a leader in the industry. These core values will allow the company to continually grow and remain an influential part of the Greenville business community.

WHNS-TV Fox 21

WHNS-TV had been on the air for about a week when the station agreed to host the Children's Miracle Network Telethon in 1984. Employees hardly knew each others' names, much less developed a sense of continuity by working together. However, the WHNS team pulled off a successful fundraising event.

Joe Heaton, Director of Programming and Creative Services who has been with the station from the beginning, says he fondly remembers that day. The foundation for WHNS-TV was built during the telethon, and it has been full steam ahead ever since.

When the station was founded in 1984, the local market, which includes the Upstate of South Carolina, Western North Carolina, and the Northeastern counties of Georgia, was the largest market (35th) in the United States without an independent TV affiliate.

Much has changed since then. When the station opened its offices on Pelham Road, it shared the area with only a few small businesses. Today, the area is booming with restaurants, hotels, banks, a movie theater, and a major international company.

In 1988, the station became an affiliate of the FOX TV Network, thus paving the way for a multitude of exciting new ventures and challenges. FOX 21 has always

Editing suite at Fox 21.

prided itself in being different from its competitors. Its programming format, which centers around young adults and families, has steadily grown in popularity with blockbuster shows such as *The Simpsons, Seinfeld, Home Improvement,* and *Friends.* When it comes to sports, the station boasts an impressive lineup including the NFL, NHL, and Major League Baseball.

"We have a more focused target audience than the other networks," Heaton says. "We can't be everything to everyone, and we know that."

In the Fall of 1996, FOX 21 entered the local news market. With its evening newscast at 10 o'clock, the station delivers the news a full hour before its competitors. The station's catch phrase is "Get it first at 10." "We felt this was a unique opportunity for us," Heaton says. "Since our target audience is young adults with families, we know a lot of them don't want to stay up until 11 o'clock to get their local news."

Due to the success of the news, the local station has plans to expand its news, weather, and sports coverage to bring the viewing audience the most compelling local and national stories, and of course, an hour before the other networks.

Through the years, FOX 21 has maintained a strong presence in the Greenville community. Many members of the station have served on the boards of civic and

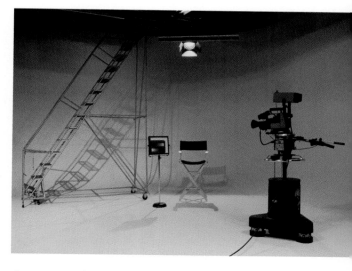

Spacious studio at Fox 21.

charitable organizations in the Greenville area. The station is also a staunch supporter of the Greenville county school district. The station's "FOX 21 Kids Club" has more than 70,000 members, which includes children through the eighth grade. A newspaper called "Kids Matter" is published 4 times a year by FOX 21, and it features the literary and artistic work of the school district's youth.

Ownership of FOX 21 changed in July 1997 when The Meredith Corporation of Des Moines, Iowa, purchased the station. However, the commitment to the local community has only grown stronger since then and will continue to do so into the future. ◖

15

Chapter Fifteen

Manufacturing and Distribution

Textube® Corporation

Textube Corporation, located on the eastern edge of Greenville County, was founded in Stamford, Conn. in 1955 as a subsidiary of Emil Adolff Spulen–and Huelsenfabrik, Reutlingen, Germany. The subsidiary company moved to the Upstate in 1968, at which time, the company's mainstay customers were in the Textile industry.

During the company's beginning stages in the Greenville area, the German-owned company specialized in manufacturing textile mill supplies such as textile yarn carriers, plastic cones, tubes, bobbins and cores for spinning, twisting, and winding of spun yarns.

Textube moved from Connecticut to the Greenville area because nearly 85 percent of its customer base was located within a 200-mile radius of the city at that time. Access to dependable transportation via I-85 and the Greenville-Spartanburg Airport was also key in determining where the company would relocate.

Much has changed since then. Greenville's economy has boomed and Textube has adjusted with the times to

Textube Corporation, located on the eastern edge of Greenville County since 1968.

meet the demands of an ever-changing global market.

Through the years Textube Corporation has continued to manufacture textile supplies, adding two-color combinations to its list of capabilities. In the 1980s, Textube diversified by making the plastic base cups for soft drink bottles, but that business discontinued when manufacturers started making one-piece bottles.

In 1991, Textube Corporation was acquired by Yazaki Industrial Chemical Co. Ltd. of Shizuoka/Japan. Yazaki designated this operation as its base to support one of its product lines—known as Creform®—in the United States.

Creform is a complete system of pipes, joints, and hardware accessories that allows companies to design and build material-handling equipment for virtually all areas of the manufacturing process. The mater-ial can be configured to meet the specific requirements of each individual company that uses the product.

Uses of Creform include racks, stands, workstations and carts, as well as conveyors, in which special channels with rollers are added to the configuration. The product has revolutionized the way manufacturers organize their operations, according

Since the company's beginning stages in the Greenville area, Textube has continued to manufacture and specialize in textile mill supplies such as textile yarn carriers, plastic cones, tubes, bobbins, and cores for spinning, twisting, and winding of spun yarns.

to Hans Freytag and Rolf Mueller, both executive vice presidents with the company.

Yazaki began making Creform in Japan more than 25 years ago, but the product wasn't introduced to the United States until the late 1980s. Today, Yazaki makes the rust-resistant pipe at its factories in Japan while Textube makes the joints, rollers, and plastic parts at Greer. Textube contracts work out for the assembly of its conveyors to the Piedmont Skills Handicap Center in Greer. Thus additional individuals are employed by Textube for 50 weeks of the year. "These individuals do quality work and by contracting out to Piedmont Skills, these individuals have the opportunity to be productive and earn money at the same time," Mueller said.

Sales of Creform parts have increased dramatically each year since the product's introduction into the United States market. The customer base of Creform includes aerospace manufacturers and electronics assemblers with food processors, health care providers, and nursery and garden supply distributors offering great potential for the future.

Despite Creform's diverse customer base, nearly two-thirds of the product is sold to automakers and their suppliers. Textube's largest customer to date is Toyota and one of its most recent sales was to supply Creform materials to the new Mercedes sport-utility vehicle plant in Vance, Alabama.

In Japan, where getting the most out of a little space is one of life's necessities, it has become popular with the general public. Not only is it widely used in Japanese factories, but it is also sold as a building block for store shelves and home projects such as rolling clothing racks and closet organizers.

Creform is helping today's manufacturers worldwide meet the challenges of a variety of global issues such as continuous productivity improvement, flexible and agile manufacturing, employee ergonomics, and green manufacturing with its global-based network of manufacturing and engineering resources.

Textube's Creform® Flow Racks play a vital role at Mercedes Benz assembly line in Tuscaloosa County, AL, production site of the ML 320 All-Activity Vehicle.

"Companies are changing processes all of the time and that's what makes Creform so special," Freytag said. It never becomes obsolete. That is if a company decides to change their material flow or manufacturing process, then Creform structures can be modified with ease to meet new needs, or you can reconfigure the material to make a new rack, stand, or workstation. Creform never has to be thrown away, thus making Creform an environmentally friendly system. "If your manufacturing process changes, then you can reconfigure the material to make a new rack, stand, or workstation."

Although the material used to make Creform is lightweight, it is sturdy enough to take on heavy loads. It also promotes organization to save valuable floor space, and it's ergonomically friendly by allowing workers to create work sites that meet their individual needs.

"Our product promotes efficiency by saving space," Freytag said. "Also, if your first-shift worker is 5-foot-2 and your second shift worker is 6-foot-5, they can both use the same workstation, because it can be easily adjusted in a couple of minutes."

Most importantly to manufacturers, according to management, is Creform promotes higher productivity in the workplace.

"Creform is a great management tool to empower employees to strive to achieve continuous improvements," Mueller said. "When you give employees the freedom to be creative, production will improve."

Textube Corporation has nearly 100 employees and future expansion is inevitable due to ever-increasing Creform sales. Textube currently has plans to expand its operation by 40,000-square-feet. About 30,000-square-feet will be manufacturing space while the additional 10,000-square-feet will be dedicated to office space and a technical center.

"Our goal is to get potential customers on site and have them build something with our product so they can see for themselves how simple it is to use Creform," Mueller said. "All of our material can be handled by ordinary people, therefore you don't need an engineering degree to put Creform materials together."

In 1996, Textube gained ISO 9002 Certification (AQA-1108). The rating is the International Quality Standard, and companies are audited on a continuous basis to assure its products and workmanship are of the highest quality possible.

Creform® is a registered trademark of Yazaki Industrial Chemical Co., Ltd.

Datastream®

Datastream® Systems, Inc. is the World Leader in Maintenance Solutions®, holding nearly half of the market share among the top 10 vendors in the computerized maintenance management systems and enterprise asset management market—including nearly two-thirds of the Fortune 500.

In 1985, Greenville's Larry Blackwell changed the face of maintenance operations. Blackwell established Datastream on the premise of helping businesses streamline their maintenance paperwork by computerizing their records. In the years since, Blackwell's vision has turned into a multi-national, multi-million dollar enterprise—Datastream Systems, with global headquarters in Greenville. By 1998, Datastream employed more than 600

Datastream's award-winning line of computerized maintenance management software has become the industry standard—garnering an unprecedented five consecutive Plant Engineering Magazine Product of the Year awards.

people and had an annual growth rate in excess of 25 percent—with a retention rate greater than most Silicon Valley technology companies.

Datastream staked an early claim in the Computerized Maintenance Management Software (CMMS) industry, believing that automation was the future for maintenance professionals. While the '80s were a graveyard for many computer interests, Blackwell recognized an entire market that virtually every other organization missed—computerized maintenance systems.

Studies indicated that companies spend an average of eight percent of their sales revenue on maintenance activities. Datastream's goal of providing easy-to-use, high-quality maintenance management software quickly found its niche—and once alliances with industry powerhouses Microsoft and Oracle were established, Datastream software quickly became the maintenance software standard.

Blackwell took the company public in 1995, trading on the NASDAQ under the symbol DSTM.

Datastream further staked its international claim with the 1996 acquisition of SQL Systems, which provided Datastream with offices in London, Paris, and Rotterdam, as well as an international distributor base in nearly 100 countries. By 1997, Datastream software had been installed in more than 40,000 sites worldwide.

While its early focus was helping companies take the first step into computerized maintenance management, as the millennium dawns, Datastream has defined a whole new category known as

Greenville's Larry Blackwell founded Datastream on the premise of helping businesses save money through computerized maintenance management software. In little more than a decade, Datastream software has been installed in 40,000 companies worldwide.

Enterprise Asset Management geared toward the specific needs of large, multi-site, multi-national corporations—particularly incorporating the power of the Internet into daily operations.

Datastream was the first to establish web-enablement as a hallmark for maintenance operations. While competitors limited the benefits of web usage to higher-end applications, Datastream developed WebLink to allow small-to-medium sized operations the ability to enjoy the low total cost of ownership inherent with web-enabled products, and to access their maintenance information from anywhere in the world via a standard web browser.

It's that visionary approach that has earned Datastream recognition as the World Leader in Maintenance Solutions. Datastream receives regular nods from the likes of *Forbes*, which named Datastream

In addition to providing cutting-edge solutions to universal maintenance needs, Datastream also offers management consulting and software training—available both on-site and at Datastream Training Centers around the world.

the 55th Best Small Company in America in 1997, and *Business Week,* which bestowed Datastream with the #5 Top Growth Company of 1996 honor. Datastream also earned an unprecedented five consecutive *Plant Engineering* Product of the Year awards.

Converting cutting-edge technology into real-world solutions, Datastream provides Windows-based maintenance solutions for operations of any size or scale.

MP5 is the world's first fully web-enabled Enterprise Asset Management solution. Geared toward the specific needs of the telecommunications, transportation, mining, and waste water treatment industries, MP5 provides unparalleled asset tracking capabilities and multiple language support for companies with high transaction volume.

MP2, available in both client/server and file-server configurations, is a corporate-wide solution that operates on the Microsoft® Access, SQL Server®, and Oracle® databases. A comprehensive Enterprise Asset Management solution, MP2's open system architecture allows for seamless integration with all major Enterprise Resource Planning (ERP) applications. In addition, MP2 provides the full spectrum of maintenance activities, including Equipment, Work Orders, and Inventory Maintenance. It also has capabilities important to today's maintenance environment, including regulatory compliance features such as audit trail, field-level security, safety notes, training records, and management reports.

Datastream's entry-level MaintainIt® offers basic maintenance functions for small businesses. MaintainIt Pro, for Windows 95 or Windows NT, offers more advanced features, such as Microsoft Office® compatibility, a drag-and-drop calendar for ease in scheduling, and Wizards to help you create work orders, purchase orders, and preventive maintenance task forms. MaintainIt Pro is also available with barcoding capabilities.

Datastream also provides cutting-edge, professional services including software customization, integration, and training, as well as management consulting such as Reliability-Centered Maintenance. To help familiarize its clients and potential customers with the vast array of software and services, Datastream maintains an informative website at www.dstm.com.

189

Datastream software is used by companies of all sizes, ranging from large, multi-national corporations needing advanced Enterprise Asset Management to small shops making the first step toward computerized maintenance management.

Ellcon-National, Inc.

When Ellcon-National, Inc. decided to relocate its corporate headquarters and manufacturing facilities in 1990, the company initiated an intensive search for a suitable location. Upon completion of the search, Greenville was at the top of the list.

Principals of Ellcon-National (left to right) Emil P. Kondra, Chairman of the Board and Douglass E. Kondra, President

The city's impressive track record of economic development and industrial growth were a major factor in the company's decision to locate in Greenville, said Douglass E. Kondra, President. Additional considerations included; state and local financial considerations, an available labor force, excellent training and technical training facilities provided by Greenville Technical College, and the quality of life.

Throughout the years, the company's growth has continued unabated with the demand for its product lines increasing annually. Therefore, expansion in the form of additional space was necessary.

Upon entering the Greenville market, Ellcon-National purchased 34 acres of land in the Beechtree Business Park located on Highway 25. The company's initial

facility was completed in August 1991 and encompassed 153,000 square-feet.

Management and the personnel at Ellcon-National have always shared an excellent relationship. Thus, when the company made its move south from New Jersey, 90 employees, including all key personnel, moved with financial assistance from the company. A short time later, ten former employees changed their minds and relocated as well.

Continued growth brought about the addition of 100,000 square-feet of additional space in 1992, and in 1997, 16.5 acres of land was purchased to build another 154,000 square-foot facility. With the additions, Ellcon-National now has more than 400,000 square-feet to handle its operations.

Ellcon-National's name, service, and products are well-known and highly respected throughout North America, Mexico, South America, Africa, and Australia.

Pre-Greenville History

The success story goes back to 1910 when William L. Conwell, Charles R. Ellicott, and J.J. Sinclair organized a company they believed would provide

substantial income for all parties involved for many years to come.

The name "Ellcon" was formed from the first three letters of Ellicott and Conwell and a Certificate of Incorporation was filed with the state of New York in 1910. The company met its objective of income-producing from the beginning, based on proper handling of employees and unwavering emphasis on product-quality, customer, and community service.

In its early stages, the company's pressing interest was in the transit industry, mainly street cars, and it was this industry the founders intended to solicit and serve. At the time, the company produced fittings, porcelain enamel stanchions, and hand holds.

In 1918, William Wampler, who had been Superintendent of the Philadelphia Transportation Company, the largest electrical railway in the world at that time, was named president of the company.

At this time, products supplied to the transit industry included fittings of all types, including stanchions and handrails, hollow metal doors for passenger and subway cars, diaphragms, window curtains, step boxes, safety step treads for steam railroad equipment, and diamond door hangers for sliding doors. Ellcon was also manufacturing and marketing oil and gas burning equipment for steamships and stationary power plants.

The company's first office was located at 165 Broadway in New York City. Some months later, it was moved into the Hudson Terminal Buildings, now the site of the World Trade Center. During this period, Mr. Wampler had invested in the National Brake Company in Buffalo, New York, a company that produced and marketed emergency hand brakes for trolley cars and freight cars. Ellcon had become the general sales agents for National Brake which supplied the transportation industry a line of emergency hand brakes known as Peacock Hand Brake, which remains the company's trademark.

In 1940, Mr. Wampler purchased The National Brake Company, and in the ensuing years, emergency hand brakes were designed for locomotives, freight cars, and

Continued growth brought about this 154,000 square-foot facility. With this addition, Ellcon-National now has more than 400,000 square-feet to handle its operations.

railroad passenger cars. This additional growth resulted in inventory and test equipment being moved to Jersey City, New Jersey, where space was allocated for this specific purpose.

Soon afterward, Emil P. Kondra was hired as a truck driver at the Jersey City facility. He soon became a "jack of all trades" and moved up the ladder quickly, while studying engineering and mechanical drawing at night to enhance his position with his new employer. He is now the company's majority owner, Chairman of the Board, and Chief Executive Officer.

During World War II, Ellcon supplied various essential parts for diesel locomotives, troop sleepers, kitchen cars, hospital cars and, as agent for Morton Manufacturing in Chicago, supplied various equipment for U.S. Navy landing craft and destroyers. At the end of hostilities, the company resumed its product manufacturing and marketing with renewed effort. At that time, a demand for hand straps, stanchions, and fittings for the New York Transit Authority developed. Ellcon responded to that demand, and this business continues to thrive.

In 1959, National Brake Company merged with Ellcon, and the business became known as it is today, Ellcon-National, Inc. Then, in 1964, Emil Kondra, who was president at the time and a coalition management employee, purchased the company. Two additional employees of that coalition remain active in the business; Robert A. Nitsch, Executive Vice President, and Mrs. Helen Perry, Corporate Secretary.

While Ellcon-National maintained small plants in New Jersey, much of its work was sub-contracted, but with new management in control and the fast growth of the organization, a plant was needed to house both executive offices and manufacturing, so the company moved to Totowa, New Jersey. It had already earned a reputation for integrity and responsibility, making its products well accepted by American, Canadian, and Mexican railroad and transit companies, to which the company extends unlimited service by its service department. That feature is perceived as the company's best product-service to

customers. Helping to promote that feature is strong, effective research and development.

A Sense of Community

Since its beginnings, Ellcon-National has always been a believer in a close-knit type organization and it values its employees' input in making the company better and stronger as it prepares for the 21st Century. Without the efforts and talents of a loyal and dedicated workforce, Ellcon-National would not be the successful company it is today.

Since relocating in Greenville, Ellcon-National has continued to enjoy great success. However, the company hasn't overlooked the importance of being a good corporate citizen. Being involved in many business, community, civic, and educational organizations has let Ellcon-National play an active role in ensuring that Greenville will be the city they anticipated back in 1990—one with the quality of life they expect and one that they now call "home." ▣

191

Ellcon-National's headquarters and manufacturing facility located in Greenville since 1991.

Collins Entertainment Corp.

Collins Entertainment Corp., headquartered in Greenville at 1341 Rutherford Road, is one of the largest privately held amusement and gaming operations in the United States.

The first brick was laid for Collins Entertainment in the 1950s when Fred Collins purchased his first jukebox for $250. Collins, CEO and sole stockholder, incorporated his amusement machine business in 1964 as Collins Music Co., Inc. The company changed its name in 1994 to Collins Entertainment Corp. Collins Entertainment has successfully conducted machine route operations from its infancy and has grown to be a leader in the amusement and gaming machine industry as a route operator and distributor.

With foresight and a diligent eye toward future trends, Collins developed the company into a statewide operation. In addition to its home office in Greenville, Collins Entertainment operates eight branch offices throughout South Carolina, including Spartanburg, Anderson, Columbia, Aiken, Florence, Charleston, Myrtle Beach, and Beaufort.

People, Equipment, and Unmatched Service

The fundamental key to success has been Collins' standards of quality, integrity, and accountability of services rendered by a knowledgeable and well-trained staff. Collins set the standards for "Instant Service" a slogan the company has proudly lived up to for four decades.

Collins offers its customers a wide variety of coin-and-currency-operated amusement and gaming machines, including the latest in video gaming devices, video arcade games, pinball machines, jukeboxes, pool tables, and novelty equipment.

Extensive research and development keep Collins Entertainment on the cutting edge of technology. Every game is protected by both internal and external security systems and accounting controls. Collins' amusement and gaming machines are engineered with security in mind and are supported by professionally managed systems to provide customers the highest standards of integrity and accountability for cash collections.

Collins' unparalleled service ethic, evidenced by "Instant Service," is founded firmly on the philosophy that profits depend on games that operate properly. Collins maintains a highly trained technical staff ready to be dispatched immediately when a problem occurs. A complete line of parts, supplies, and specialty diagnostic equipment ensures immediate repair service.

Fred Collins, CEO and Sole Stockholder

The driving force behind the Collins organization is Fred Collins, an entrepreneur with a history of innovation, drive, and success. Collins takes a direct interest in the daily operations of Collins Entertainment Corp. and its affiliates. His drive and energy is imparted to all members of the Collins team, ensuring the success of each new venture.

With more than 35 years of experience, Collins is recognized as a leader in the coin operated amusement and gaming machine industry. He is a member and past president of the industry's national trade association, Amusement and Music Operators Association (AMOA). He served on the first educational committee and helped design and develop the industry's Executive Development Program held at Notre Dame University. Over the years, Collins has conducted numerous educational seminars at the AMOA national conventions.

Fred Collins is active in community service and serves on several advisory boards, including the Greenville Tech Foundation, the University of South Carolina Law School Partnership, and CrimeStoppers of Greenville. In 1987, he was appointed a commissioner for the Commission on the Future of South Carolina.

The Fred Collins Foundation, a private charitable organization, was established by Collins in 1986 to improve and stimulate growth in education and the arts in South Carolina, and to support other charitable causes.

Collins Entertainment is recognized not

Fred Collins, Founder and CEO of Collins Entertainment. Photo by Martin Nubson/Ernest Rawlins Photography.

Collins Entertainment offers a wide variety of amusements–finding the perfect game for any taste. Photo by Martin Nubson.

enterprises, real estate, a marina, and a casino cruise ship. These affiliated companies operate in South Carolina, Georgia, Florida, Kentucky, Indiana, Louisiana, Colorado, New York, Montana, and Wisconsin.

Today, Collins Entertainment Corp. and affiliates maintain a total of 21 branch locations supported by 480 employees. Every member of the Collins team challenges themselves to strive for increased sales, better customer service, and greater professionalism. Employees of Collins Entertainment Corp. and its affiliates know that by grasping opportunities and by realizing goals they can build on the tradition started back in 1964.

The Collins organization offers years of experience, a large well-trained staff, the financial resources of a successful company, and management expertise resulting in professional and profitable operation of coin operated amusement and gaming machines. ⌐

only as a leader in the coin-operated amusement and gaming industry, but also as a partner in the communities where the company does business. Collins has a long history of community involvement through support of community, educational, and charitable organizations. A fundamental focus of Collins is the betterment of those communities that have become home to the company and its employees.

(l-r) J. Marshall Armstrong, Vice President of Operations and James G. Tzouvelekas, Vice President of Finance. Photo by Martin Nubson/Ernest Rawlins Photography.

Company Growth

Succeeding in today's complex amusement and entertainment industry requires an approach that embraces innovation, integrity, and attention to detail, the foundation upon which Collins Entertainment Corp. is built.

As gaming acceptability has spread throughout the U.S., Fred Collins and his affiliated companies have followed opportunities into new jurisdictions. In addition to Collins Entertainment Corp., Collins has affiliated entities operating in nine states throughout the U.S., including not only amusement and gaming machine route operations, but also bowling center

193

Perrigo Company of South Carolina

Rod Hochmuth, VP of Operations states, "Perrigo in Greenville, SC is a leading nutritional private label manufacturing facility. The recent volatile growth in the nutritional market has allowed us to significantly expand our facility and workforce. Being in Greenville has allowed this growth to happen easily with an excellent source of responsible associates."

Perrigo Company is the nation's largest manufacturer of over-the-counter (non-prescription) pharmaceutical, personal care, and nutritional products for the store brand market. Store-brand products are sold under a retailer's own label and compete with nationally advertised brand name products.

Perrigo's mission is to deliver quality products and services at the lowest total cost while exceeding each customer's expectations. With some of the most knowledgeable and proficient associates in the industry and by developing long-term relationships with customers, Perrigo is delivering store brand value to both retailers and consumers.

By excelling in all areas, from manufacturing and distribution to quality and customer service, Perrigo has become the leading U.S. producer of store brand health and beauty care products. Perrigo's manufacturing expertise has been a key ingredient to the company's success in the very cost-competitive store-brand market. Perrigo uses its manufacturing skills to deliver quality products at competitive prices. In every step of the manufacturing process, from raw material analysis to packaging, Perrigo strives for excellence. The company ensures every product meets stringent specifications including state and national standards and guidelines while maintaining a high level of service.

The company's customers consist of major national and regional retail drug, supermarket, mass merchandise chains, and major wholesalers. The company's products include over-the-counter pharmaceuticals such as analgesics, cough and cold remedies, antacids, laxatives, suppositories, feminine hygiene, and diet products; personal care products such as toothpaste and mouthwash, hair care products, "wets," baby care products, and skin and sun care products; and nutritional products such as vitamins, nutritional supplements, and nutritional drinks.

Perrigo offers a diverse line of more than 900 items that provide unlimited opportunities in markets throughout the world. The key to success has been offering consumer quality and value while still being able to offer a higher profit margin for retailers. Consumers reap the benefits of the store-brand products because Perrigo products are comparable in quality and effectiveness to favorite name brands, but are available at substantial savings.

Today, Perrigo of South Carolina has developed into a major nutritional manufacturing facility. At present, the business

Randy Kearse, Blending associate, prepares the 150 cubic foot blender for raw materials.

Packaging associate, Tammy Waters, inspects private label vitamins.

Patricia Blanton, Microbiologist, records product data from Micro assays.

manufactures and distributes private and control label natural and synthetic vitamins, minerals, and other nutritional products that are sold nationally and internationally through major chain drug stores, supermarkets, and mass merchandise outlets.

Previously known as Bell Pharmacal Corporation, the company began as Table Rock Laboratories, Inc. and was organized on June 1, 1927. Dr. George R. Wilkinson and Dr. I.S. Barksdale, two local Greenville physicians founded the company. The company operated out of a store building on Brown Street for the first few years and then moved to Hampton Avenue.

In 1950, Charlie Bell joined the company as Assistant Manager and became President in 1951. Through his efforts, the ownership of the company was changed to the common stockholders and the name was officially changed to Bell Pharmacal in 1969 even though it continued to be referred to as Table Rock Labs for several years. In late 1971, the company moved to its present location at 4615 Dairy Drive off I-85. In 1972, the company became affiliated with the Kroger Company of Cincinnati, Ohio and in 1984, the facility became part of Perrigo Company.

In 1887, Luther Perrigo, operator of an apple-drying business and general store near Allegan, Michigan, began repackaging and distributing patent medicine to rural general stores. Business grew and by the early 1920s as many as 50 Perrigo Company route salesmen were calling on the rural trade. From 1920 to 1950, the company made a transition in the market place, moving from rural stores to chain stores.

Perrigo operates eleven manufacturing

facilities today, which occupy more than two million square feet. In addition to the Greenville operation are their personal care operations in St. Louis, Missouri; Smyrna, Tennessee; and Bernardino, California. OTC pharmaceuticals are manufactured at six sites in Allegan, Holland, and Montague, Michigan. In 1997, Perrigo added to its manufacturing facilities by acquiring 88 percent interest in Quimica y Farmacia, S.A. de C.V., a Mexican pharmaceutical manufacturer and distributor.

Much has changed at Perrigo Company since Luther Perrigo founded it in 1887. Yet one fact remains the same. Then as now, the company is known for delivering value—high quality products at a low cost. ◖

PYA/Monarch, Inc.

P YA/Monarch, Inc. is the largest food-service distributor in the Southeast, with annual sales exceeding $2.4 billion. PYA/Monarch maintains 14 branches, supplying produce, fresh and frozen meat, fish and poultry, dairy products, canned goods, non-foods and disposables, and small wares to restaurants, hotels, clubs, schools, health care organizations, and major fast food chains.

A Long History in the Foodservice Industry

In 1903, C.C. Pearce founded the Pearce-Young-Angel Company (PYA) in Columbia, S.C. to supply fresh fruit and vegetables to retail grocery stores. 23 years later, C.C. Pearce, Jr. opened the Greenville branch of PYA. The gap from grocery store sales to foodservice distribution was bridged when PYA began supplying local hotels and eateries.

PYA entered the foodservice market in 1939. Considering the relatively underdeveloped foodservice industry at the time, it was a daring move. Still, the market held interesting potential since there were few sources of supply for operators. Most food retailers were buying from absentee distributors and paying extraordinarily high prices.

First In Foodservice

Initially, PYA offered produce and institutional canned products, grocery specialties, and dried fruits and vegetables. That list was expanded in 1937, when PYA became the first distributor in the Carolinas to stock frozen foods, as well as the first forwarding warehouse in the area. That same year, the company took another innovative step, forming an advanced sales force when other distributors were selling right off the truck.

The foodservice business was climbing, and PYA began to phase out all of its retail trade. The process was slow, but by the end of the 1960s, the firm was involved almost exclusively in the foodservice industry.

Today, the Monarch name represents one of the oldest national foodservice companies in the United States. Reid,

Murdoch, Inc., which became a part of Consolidated Foods Corporation in 1956, once supplied goods for the wagon trains heading west back in 1859. Their products were packed under the nationally known Monarch brand name, the oldest foodservice brand in the country.

In 1967, PYA merged with Consolidated Foods (now Sara Lee Corporation), and the longtime Greenville company joined with Monarch to become PYA/Monarch, Inc.

An Integrity-Driven Organization

PYA/Monarch is an organization of integrity—integrity of person, of purpose, and of products. The product offerings span all varieties of foods and non-foods under the Monarch brand and other nationally branded products.

PYA/Monarch offers its customers trained sales representatives and specialists to assist with menu planning, pricing, and nutritional information via state-of-the-art laptop computers. Additional assistance includes updates on market conditions and new product demonstrations.

Through its mission statement, the company endeavors to achieve market dominance and profitable growth by demonstrating a clear understanding of all its customers' needs. Employees of PYA/Monarch work with and for their customers, providing goods and services needed to help customers achieve profitable growth as well.

Community Involvement

Involvement in the Greenville community closely parallels the interests of PYA/Monarch

employees. The company is a major sponsor of local fine arts and educational programs, and its community service is not limited to monetary donations. Employees are actively encouraged to participate in blood drives, the Literacy Association, March of Dimes Walk America, and the annual United Way campaign. The employees also have a special Christmas program throughout the year that enables them to sponsor needy families.

A Base in Greenville

The company's initial location in Greenville was at its warehouse at 490 McBee Avenue. That facility was part of the old Piedmont and Northern Warehouse Complex until 1960, when the company moved to a new location on White Horse Road. Today, PYA/Monarch's headquarters are located in Greenville. The company's 4,000 employees serve their customer base through its distribution facilities throughout the Southeast and Midwest. [◄]

Hoechst Diafoil

Hoechst Diafoil Co. is part of one of the world's largest polyester companies, a joint venture partnership among Hoechst Celanese, Hoechst AG of Germany, and Japan's Mitsubishi Chemical. The 190-acre site in Greer is the administrative, manufacturing, research and development, and marketing headquarters for production of Hostaphan® polyester film.

Hoechst Diafoil Co. manufactures top quality polyester film that is used in many areas of everyday life. Hostaphan polyester film goes into reprographic uses such as engineering film, graphic arts, transparency film, and digital printing. Packaging uses include printed, metallized, laminated packaging, and clear labels. Electrical uses involve wire and cable insulation. There are many industrial uses including solar/safety window film, release film, label and decal, roll leaf, thermal laminations, flexible duct, and other building products.

Building the Work Force of Tomorrow

Realizing the students of today are the workforce of tomorrow, Hoechst Diafoil is actively involved in the Greenville County School District's Business Education Partnership.

"Hoechst Diafoil is dedicated to the education of our young people," says Carly Culbertson, director of the Business Education Partnership. "Hoechst not only encourages their employees to be active participants in the education system, they allow them to take time out of the work day to go out and talk with students and visit the schools."

The company sponsors several nearby schools, and Hoechst employees participate at nearly every school and grade level district-wide through programs such as tutoring, middle school shadowing, 11th-grade shadowing, volunteer speaking, Junior Achievement, and a Summer Internship Program for high school juniors and seniors.

Each school year, new high school students are invited to tour part of the Hoechst Diafoil plant so they can witness some of the everyday miracles of chemistry and engineering. "Hoechst is really big on math and science, and they believe once students see the practical application of those subjects, many of them become more interested in pursuing a career in either of those fields."

Through the years, numerous employees and Hoechst Diafoil have earned countless community service awards for their work with the school district. The awards and recognition are special, but Hoechst and its employees know the development of tomorrow's workforce and ensuring their future is more important than any individual or company award.

"The employees of Hoechst Diafoil are positively influencing our youth, and we'll be better off in the future and have a well-trained workforce thanks to companies like Hoechst playing such an active role in our partnership," Culbertson said.

Concern For Company and Community

Hoechst Diafoil is equally concerned with the workforce of nearly 900 employees and contractors; the company is one of the largest employers in Greenville County.

Betty Holcombe, president of the Greer Chamber of Commerce, says Hoechst Diafoil has provided good paying jobs for

The sophisticated polyester film and resins production process takes place at the company's 190 acre site in Greer. The plant also has its own polymer manufacturing units and a full complement of support facilities.

the citizens of Greer and has constantly expanded throughout the years, thus ensuring the economic stability of the area. ⦿

Lockheed Martin Aircraft & Logistics Centers

Commercial airline and defense customers around the world are seeking extended life for their aging aircraft fleets. They need a single point of support for all their maintenance, modification, and logistics requirements—a company as dependable as the laws of aerodynamics.

That company is Lockheed Martin Aircraft & Logistics Centers (LMALC). The company has relished the opportunity to refurbish a variety of aircraft fleets, and continues to compete for contracts around the world.

On January 1, 1997, Lockheed Martin Corporation selected the Upstate as the home for the headquarters of its newest international company. LMALC was created through the consolidation of four Lockheed Martin Aeronautics Sector operating units including the Lockheed Martin Aircraft Center in Greenville. LMALC has approximately 8,000 employees and operates more than 90 sites and facilities around the globe.

International Presence

LMALC is engaged in providing aircraft maintenance, modification, logistics support, and aerostructures manufacturing for both commercial and military customers. The company's core businesses include its Aircraft Center at Greenville; an aerostructures facility in Baltimore; logistics management operations at 80 sites around the world; and international operations in Budapest, Hungary; Cordoba, Argentina; Guanzhou, China; Hamilton, New Zealand; and in Saudi Arabia.

The company's strategy for growth involves making its services more attractive to customers by expanding core businesses to achieve total support capability. The corporation's acquisition of Northrop Grumman is expected to improve that capability, bringing complimentary facilities under the company's control.

In short, LMALC is one company that customers can depend on to provide maximum lift and zero drag.

Greenville Aircraft Center

Located at the Donaldson Center Industrial Air Park since 1984, the Aircraft Center provides total contractor logistics support with an emphasis on heavy aircraft for commercial and defense customers. Currently, the center is successfully performing aircraft depot maintenance contracts for the Air Force KC-10, and Navy P-3 and C-9 aircraft. The center also conducted maintenance and modifications services for commercial carriers such as Delta, Federal Express, UPS, and Northwest.

The center encompasses 161 acres with 14 hangers and 26 fully-equipped bays offering the full spectrum of aircraft maintenance services from large structural repairs to engine changes, passenger/freighter conversions, flight control changes, airframe overhaul, and interior refurbishment.

Commercial Modifications

The center is also geared to conduct Lockheed Martin L-1011 TriStar freighter conversions under an agreement with Marshall Aerospace, based in the United Kingdom.

The center performs its services to the most exacting standards in the industry, including services related to VIP,

Greenville Aircraft Center technicians provide quality support for military and commercial aircraft.

LMALC engineers use state-of-the-art technology to provide the solutions that put customers' aircraft back in the sky.

head-of-state, and special air mission aircraft. The center has always been guided by simple precepts: offer the highest levels of craftsmanship and services possible, meet or beat schedule needs, and perform the job at a competitive price. 🖘

T&S Brass and Bronze Works, Inc.

With a steadfast commitment to quality, T&S Brass and Bronze Works, Inc. has set the standard of excellence for the plumbing industry for half a century.

Founded in 1947, T&S originally developed foodservice plumbing equipment, including the markets first pre-rinse unit, which became the industry standard. Then in 1950, the company introduced its full line of foodservice plumbing products and T&S was established as the premiere manufacturer in the industry. By 1953, T&S had introduced the foot pedal valve, yet another product that became the industry standard.

In 1956, T&S made its debut in the laboratory market with its Lab-Flo line of laboratory service fittings. Four years later, the company expanded into non-residential markets with industrial-grade faucets for institutional applications, and penetration of the commercial plumbing market began.

More than 30 years after building a successful business on Long Island, NY, T&S moved its company headquarters in 1978 to Travelers Rest, just north of Greenville. The current location, which employs nearly 250 people, manufactures products and services customers.

Throughout the years, T&S has continued to enter new markets within the plumbing industry. Today, the company produces faucets, fittings, and specialty products for foodservice, industrial, commercial plumbing, and laboratory markets. Its products have become the standard for the majority of U.S. hospitals, schools, restaurants, prisons, and public facilities.

The T&S expansion, however, has not been limited to the borders of the United States. During the last 20 years, the company has significantly increased its overseas exports. Today, representatives sell T&S products in Europe, Australia, the Middle East, Canada, Japan, Asia, and South America.

In addition to the company's headquarters in Travelers Rest, T&S has a second U.S. distribution center in Simi Valley, California. To support its growing global distribution system, T&S has established facilities on several continents including overseas offices and distribution centers located in Europe, Australia, and Asia.

As a leader in quality manufacturing, T&S proudly displays the certification of both the International Organization for Standardization (ISO) and NSF International. These certifications demonstrate that T&S consistently delivers the quality products and services on which its customers depend.

T&S is a leader in the local community as well when it comes to community service and environmental awareness.

In the Greenville community, T&S supports local public schools, Furman University and Greenville Technical College. The company contributes financially to many worthwhile causes, and donates necessities such as shower equipment, faucets, and other plumbing equipment to charities and children's shelters on a regular basis.

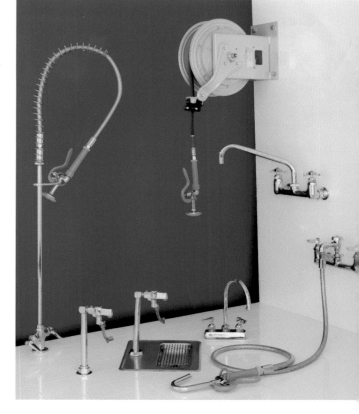

T&S, as a company, and its employees are committed to a clean and safe environment through a rigid recycling program. T&S recycles everything from soda cans to boxes, shipping materials, and metal scraps and shavings.

The company's efforts haven't gone unnoticed. T&S received the Governor's Pollution Prevention Award in 1991 and Manufacturer of the Year from the Greenville Chamber of Commerce in 1992. Also, the Western Carolina Regional Sewer Authority presented T&S with the Best Pollution Prevention Program Award in 1994 and the Compliance Excellence Award in 1995. ◖

199

Rockwell Automation/Dodge

B ack in 1881, in a small factory in Mishawaka, Indiana, Wallace Dodge invented the revolutionary "Independence Split Wood Pulley." This unique pulley was the beginning of what would soon become a rich history of pioneering innovation and manufacturing excellence by a leader in mechanical power transmission solutions.

For more than 120 years, DODGE has been one of the leading suppliers of mechanical power transmission products and systems components in the world. Today, it is a business unit of Rockwell Automation.

Since 1985, Rockwell has made substantial investments in its automation business, weaving brands like DODGE into its fold—brands that include Allen-Bradley, Reliance Electric, and Rockwell Software. As part of this Rockwell Automation family, DODGE has the capability to leverage its industrial automation expertise and focus its efforts on diversified solutions for its customers.

To this end, DODGE employs more

than 3,200 people worldwide. It operates 11 ISO 9002-certified manufacturing facilities, 13 distribution facilities, and more than 100 sales offices located in eight countries. Within its facilities, DODGE manufactures industry-proven, high-performance DODGE®, MASTER®, and REEVES® products, including mounted bearings, gear reducers, mechanical adjustable speed drives, shaft-mounted reducers, conveyor pulleys, shaft couplings, bushings, clutches, and motor brakes. These products are in use today throughout the world in aggregate, mining, automotive, food processing, timber processing, and pulp and paper industries.

Competing on an international basis, DODGE continuously strives to create the world's most successful customers and suppliers. It establishes win-win

Preparing USAF Roller Bearing Housings for shipment at the Rogersville Plant.

relationships, and is dedicated to meeting their demands for the highest quality and best selection of power transmission products, systems, and support in the industry.

Closer to home, DODGE is equally committed to the economic growth and well-being of the Upstate communities. It actively demonstrates a company-wide commitment to the United Way, and is a recognized force in Leadership Greenville and the Chamber of Commerce.

Innovation. Feature-rich products. Responsive sales and support. Community involvement. These are ways in which DODGE is focused on being the global leader in mechanical power transmission and ways in which it is committed to making its customers and the Upstate successful.

Assembly of a REEVES® MOTO DRIVE at the Reeves Plant.

Hitachi Electronic Devices (USA), Inc.

In late 1989, Hitachi decided Greenville was a prime location to construct its only tube plant in the United States. Thus, Hitachi Electronic Devices (USA), Inc. was established in February 1990, and the intersection of I-85 and Mauldin Road was chosen as the plant site.

After looking at many sites on the East Coast and across the Southeast, Hitachi determined Greenville was the sensible choice for the plant. Factors attributing to Hitachi's decision were the site's proximity to potential customers, cooperation of local and state government, the pro-business stance of the community, an abundant water supply, and a qualified labor force.

The plant's initial products were color picture tubes (CPT). Construction of the plant began on April 20, 1990, and CPT production began on November 13, 1991. Construction on an addition to the facility started in September 1993 to accommodate a new product line: projection ray tubes (PRT). PRT production began September 2, 1994.

Hitachi Electronic Devices is situated on a 53.5 acre site and encompasses approximately 600,000 square feet. Nearly 1,100 full-time employees work at the plant, which operates 24 hours a day, seven days per week. The majority of the employees work on the manufacturing

Hitachi Electronic Devices (USA), Inc. Manufacturing plant in Greenville, South Carolina.

line while a support group of managers, engineers, and technical specialists round out the team.

The production of the local plant's CPTs range from 27" to 32". Hitachi's CPTs are full square screens with optimized panel curvature, making the tubes optimally designed and well suited to various modern TV designs. The CPTs are used in Hitachi televisions as well as those of other TV manufacturers worldwide.

Production of the CPTs is an advanced process requiring the highest levels of technology, precise engineering skills, and highly sophisticated equipment.

Hitachi's PRTs feature a direct optical coupling system that creates images with exceptionally high resolution and superb highlight brightness. These remarkable capabilities make them ideal for projection TV applications.

The products produced at the Greenville plant are backed by Hitachi's many years of experience in the electronics industry. A team of dedicated engineers ensures the highest levels of quality and reliability, so all products fully meet the expectations of customers worldwide.

Quality always comes first at Hitachi. Therefore, all Hitachi products undergo

Section of the Hitachi manufacturing plant where the products undergo the quality assurance test.

rigorous inspection standards. Consistently, Hitachi CPTs and PRTs receive worldwide recognition for the highest quality available. And, with the future of television moving toward digital and high definition models, Hitachi will be at the forefront as these advanced technologies move into the worldwide market.

Hitachi Electronic Devices is also committed to environmental controls. That's why the company has a sophisticated on-site system providing a full range of utilities to support its complicated manufacturing processes. A specially designed water treatment plant is in place to preserve a clean environment.

In the areas of corporate citizenship, community service, and employee activity, Hitachi is a recognized leader. From support of Freedom Weekend Aloft, Junior Achievement, the United Way, local hospice programs, and School to Work Education programs to employee softball, bowling, and golf, Hitachi Electronic Devices and its employees carry on the tradition of community service and employee activity.

201

BMW

When BMW made the landmark decision to locate a manufacturing facility in the United States, the company chose a 1,039-acre site in Upstate South Carolina as its new home after examining more than 250 possible locations worldwide.

As one of five factories within BMW's production system, the $1.2 billion investment is key to BMW's standing as a global vehicle manufacturer.

South Carolina was selected because of its easily accessible transportation facilities, including Charleston's deep-water port, its strong commitment to help new and existing industries train workers, and an available workforce with a strong work ethic.

Plant construction began in April 1993 and the first American-made BMW was shipped to a customer in March 1995, marking the fastest start-up in automobile manufacturing industry. Unlike many other automobile factories, all of the manufacturing processes are under one roof, creating an open communications environment that enhances the focus on quality.

The BMW Zentrum is a visitors center and display facility that serves as a site for community meetings and conferences.

After the first year of operations, a decision was implemented to expand the plant increasing production capacity from 300 to 400 units per day by the year 2000.

More than 2,000 associates work at BMW and locating the plant in the United States has led to the creation of a North American supplier network encompassing 100 companies and at least 22 suppliers have chosen to locate in South Carolina within a few hours drive of the plant.

One of the most striking features of the facility is the BMW Zentrum, a visitors center and display facility that communicates BMW's heritage of engineering excellence, innovation, and commitment to social responsibility.

Four separate but integrated galleries give visitors a view of BMW's contributions in engineering, environmental quality, manufacturing excellence, and cultural enrichment.

A special section of the Zentrum features a display on the world-renown BMW Art Cars, which have been painted by internationally recognized artists, such as Andy Warhol, Roy Lichenstein, Esther Mahlangua, Sandro Chio, and David Hockney. The connection between automotive technology and the art world

A fireworks display celebrates the grand opening of BMW Manufacturing Corp. in November, 1994.

began in 1975 when artist Alexander Calder painted the first art car.

Through the Virtual Factory Tour film, spectators experience the sensation of being on the manufacturing line as a BMW is built and gives them a car's eye view of how a BMW comes together.

The Zentrum serves as a bridge between BMW and the community, serving as a site for meetings and conferences on economic development, tourism, the arts, lifestyle and education, as well as the automobile industry.

The company is committed to being a responsible corporate citizen, beginning with a plant designed with environmental safety and protection as prime considerations.

The goal is to produce automobiles of the highest quality while at the same time having the minimum impact on the environment.

BMW is active in contributing to the educational, cultural, environmental, and social life of South Carolina and its people. 🖘

South Carolina Steel Corporation

Since its founding in 1952, South Carolina Steel Corporation has played a major role in Greenville's growth and development. The corporation has grown to be the largest steel fabricator in the region, employing more than 170 people and fabricating more than 30,000 tons of steel annually.

Although South Carolina Steel has a variety of the most technologically advanced equipment in the industry today, the corporation's people are the real reason for its success. Their can-do attitude and "It's got to be right" mindset have earned a loyal customer base. Training and motivating employees to build quality products at low prices, which customers desire, is at the heart of South Carolina Steel's mission.

The management philosophy is based upon the Golden Rule, and the work environment is similar to that of a close-knit family. Relations with fellow employees are governed by the following principles: the dignity of the individual, mutual respect, the importance of the supervisor, and the profit motive.

Loyalty is the cornerstone of the business. The corporation's steel fabricators average nine years of service, and over 50 percent have five or more years of service. Likewise, the business benefits from a loyal customer base, with more than 70 percent of the work being repeat business. South Carolina Steel values a loyal and effective base of suppliers who play a key role in maintaining the corporation's reputation in the industry.

In 1994, South Carolina Steel merged with Dallas-based Commercial Metals Company. This affiliation not only gives South Carolina Steel one of the strongest balance sheets in the steel fabrication industry, but also makes it part of a network of rolling mills and fabrication shops spanning from coast to coast.

South Carolina Steel has furnished steel for several Greenville landmarks, including BMW, Michelin, Kemet Electronics, Caterpillar, Alfmeier Corporation, Haywood Mall, Greenville Hyatt and Commons, Peace Center, BI-LO Center, Greenville Hospital System, St. Francis Hospital, and Furman University, among others.

The corporation's work is not limited to Greenville. As customers have broadened

The Shriner's Hospital is just one of many Greenville landmarks built using South Carolina Steel products.

203

South Carolina Steel's friendly drivers have the best safety record in the more than 50-year history of the Steel Group. Like their fellow employees, they don't just get the job done; they get the job done right!

their horizons, they have taken South Carolina Steel with them throughout the United States, Canada, Puerto Rico, Saudi Arabia, and Japan.

The South Carolina Steel "Family of Fabricators" has been a solid member of the Greenville community for more than 45 years and will continue to play a role in its growth and development for many years to come.

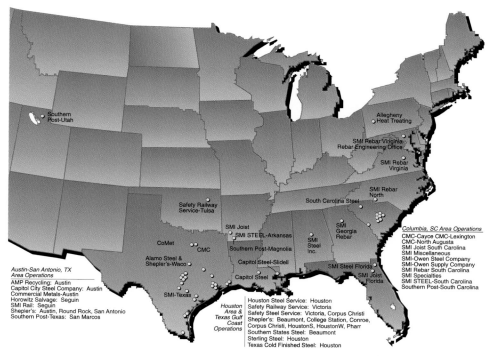

The CMC Steel Group is a worldwide leader in manufacturing, marketing, and recycling steel. As a member of the Steel Group, South Carolina Steel not only enjoys financial strength, but also is part of a network of fabricators and mills spanning throughout the United States.

The Cline Company

From its inception as a one-man company operating from a small house located at 5 Atwood Street in downtown Greenville in 1948, The Cline Company has grown to more than 80 employees and into facilities exceeding 80,000 square-feet today.

Now celebrating their *50th Anniversary,* the company has built its success around some basic principles—providing quality products and services to its customers.

Founded by N. Q. Cline Sr., The Cline Company is located in a multi-building complex on Buncombe Street. Throughout the years, the company has remained family-owned. Cline Sr. serves as the company's President and treasurer, his wife Martha A. Cline serves as Vice President and secretary, while their sons David M. Cline Sr. and N. Q. Cline Jr. each serve as Vice Presidents.

Currently, The Cline Company serves a variety of markets with a wide-range of products such as clutches, drivelines, hydraulic hoses and cylinders, valves, pumps, brakes, and power take-offs. These products are used in the paper, steel, and marine industries as well as for earth-moving equipment such as bull-dozers, front-end loaders, cranes, shovels, and hoist equipment.

The Hose and Hydraulics Division fabricates hydraulic hoses from single wire to six spiral wire. It also supplies both bronze and stainless steel hose assemblies for water, steam, and truck transfer applications.

The Cline Company consists of three divisions, all located within walking distance of each other at 600 Buncombe Street: the main office and manufacturing facility of the mill products division (pictured here), the hose and hydraulic division, and the mobile products division (not pictured).

The Cline Company, which began as a one-man operation, is now a family-run company that is three generations strong. Standing: (left to right) N.Q. Cline Sr., Founder, David M. Cline Sr., N.Q. Cline Jr., David M. Cline Jr. Seated: (left to right) Wade S. Cline, Martha A. Cline, Glenn M. Cline, Scott N. Cline.

The Mobile Products Division supplies transmissions, clutches, drivelines, brakes, control cables, hydraulic cylinders, valves, pumps, and power take-off components/assemblies for the automotive, truck, and mobile off-highway markets.

The Cline Company also operates a Mill Products Division, which sells clutches, driveshafts, and complete braking systems—both air and water cooled—for use in industrial plants. These mill products are original Cline designs and are fabricated at their extensive in-house machine shop.

Customer service has always been the cornerstone of The Cline Company. According to Cline Sr., the company's commitment to its customers has kept the company in business while allowing for long-term client relationships to flourish. This commitment explains how the company has retained all of its initial customers, who are still in business today, as present customers.

As for new technologies, the company's engineering department remains on the cutting edge by continually developing new products and improving old ones. The Cline Company manufacturers state-of-the-art equipment in-house as well as rebuilding and repairing almost every type of clutch, brake, universal driveshaft, or gear coupling available.

The company also maintains an extensive inventory of more than 10,000 line-item components from raw to semi-finished and finished material to meet the fast turnaround its customers require.

Mr. Cline is quick to point out the company's employees and associates have been their greatest asset. The company has built an outstanding reputation in the community and among its customer base which reaches nationwide as well as across Europe and Asia.

The Cline Company is also committed to the well-being and growth of the Greenville area. This is expressed through their continued support of the United Way, the Greater Greenville Chamber of Commerce, the Salvation Army, Shepherd's Gate, Miracle Hill, and the Rescue Mission.

As for the future, The Cline Company plans to tackle the next 50 years as it has its first half-century—commitment to quality products, superior customer service, and dedication to emerging technologies. ◄

Package Supply & Equipment Co., Inc.

Consistent growth and increasing profits best define Package Supply & Equipment Co., Inc. (PSE), which began as a one person, one office operation in 1967. During the past 30 years, the company has grown to 130 employees and seven facilities east of the Mississippi River.

The company's president, Gary Daniels, says he couldn't have selected a better location than Greenville to start a business. The fast-growing economy, as well as the city's location along I-85 between Atlanta and Charlotte have contributed to the company's success.

Throughout the years, PSE has supported the arts, education, law enforcement, and many other worthwhile causes in Greenville and the state of South Carolina.

Personally, Mr. Daniels has served on the boards at the Greater Greenville Chamber of Commerce, University of South Carolina Endowment Fund, Camp Greenville, YMCA, National Association of Container Distributors, Buncombe Street United Methodist Church, USC-Spartanburg, Columbia College, and the former

(l-r) Gary Daniels, Jr., Vice President of Operations, Tom Toler, Vice President of Sales, Gary Daniels, Sr., President.

South Carolina National Bank.

In addition to two Greenville facilites, the company has facilities in Atlanta, Charlotte, Nashville, Cincinnati, and Newark.

As a "Packaging" leader in the United States, PSE works hand-in-hand with its many customers to develop new and fresh concepts through its art and design department. Once creative design and renderings are agreed upon, PSE sends the materials to its marketing department for package development. When the customer likes a design or suggestion by PSE, a prototype design is delivered for consideration.

At PSE, concepts, materials, and technologies all proliferate nearly as fast as the new product packaging they are designed to serve.

Perhaps the climate of incessant change is responsible for the ethic that runs so deep within the corporate culture of PSE. It is an ethic where information and logistics management, linked to a broad array of technical services, are as important as packaging "hardware." Indeed, knowing the materials, technology, laws, trends, and performing services packagers require is what separates an industry leader from just another supplier.

Even a quick glance at Package Supply's product catalog demonstrates the company's commitment to meeting the diverse needs of today's packagers. More than 20,000 items are portrayed in the catalog's 125 pages,

Corporate Headquarters, Greenville, South Carolina.

showcasing every imaginable style, size, and material of rigid containers and closures. Containers include glass and plastic bottles, tubes, tubs, jars, and pails. Closure offerings are available in simple snap-ons, convenience closures, tamper-evident closures, sprayers, dispensers, and many other accessories designed to fit a specific need.

Of particular pride at PSE is the company's information system, one of the most advanced in accessing product, production, and logistic information. A variety of management information reports can be customized to provide customers with the data managers need to make better decisions. With seven facilities tied into the network, PSE employees can synchronize production schedules with logistic needs. PSE has been a pioneer in introducing electronic data interchange (EDI), giving customers the ability to link their computers to PSE for immediate inventory, order and shipment status.

In short, combining formidable product lines with cutting-edge technical service allows PSE to address each customer's requirements throughout packaging supply chains. Integrating concept development with inventory management and considering all aspects including recycling and many other issues, PSE provides its customers with no less than "the total package."

As in the past, PSE will go into the 21st century a leader in the sales and distribution of rigid containers and closures. ◻

205

Alfmeier Corporation

Launching Alfmeier's first North American manufacturing facility in 1995 was only the beginning for this corporate team which continues to meet every challenge thrust at a fast growing automotive supplier. Sales have increased by more than 500 percent in fewer than four years, and Alfmeier Corporation has distinguished itself as a world-class supplier of fuel system products and valves for the global automotive industry.

Alfmeier's North American manufacturing facility and headquarters, based in Greenville, is a subsidiary of German-based Alfmeier Präzision AG, which brings more than 30 years of experience to the automotive industry. The company's local state-of-the-art 30,000 square foot production facility operates 24 hours a day, six days a week, and is supported by an engineering division in Troy, Michigan.

Alfmeier supplies fuel management systems and fuel system components to BMW and to Mercedes-Benz. Other customers include Kautex, Plastic Omnium, Solvay Automotive, Pierburg, AFCO, Pilot Industries, and ITT for product applications at Chrysler, Honda, Mitsubishi, and Ford, as well as other OEM customers.

Alfmeier Corporation's capabilities include designing, manufacturing, and supplying sophisticated fuel management systems for fuel tanks; a variety of fuel system components and valves; vapor-venting devices; and other automotive applications for North American and European automakers, along with new opportunities being pursued in South America and Asia.

While experiencing tremendous growth in its brief history, Alfmeier Corporation has already achieved several milestones including participating in numerous product development "hot-trip" tests in Arizona sponsored by Chrysler, GM, Kautex, and Solvay; acceptance of patent applications for new products including the company's Onboard Refueling Vapor Recovery (ORVR) system; development of a "zero-leak" valve; and more than doubling its number of employees in the United States over the past year. The parent organization in Germany likewise continues to grow and strengthen its financial resources to support Alfmeier's global expansion opportunities.

Today, signs of well-managed, aggressive growth are evident at Alfmeier. "Key technical positions and experience add strength to Alfmeier's team which has enabled the company to rapidly develop into a world-class automotive production facility," says Sam Konduros, Executive Vice President for North America.

"A seasoned team of veterans, like the one we have in place, is a significant investment for a company the size of Alfmeier," says Konduros. "But, Alfmeier is committed to the North American market for the long term, and this powerful team will help us achieve our ultimate goal—to be the North American market leader in fuel system valves and a true expert in fuel management systems."

Alfmeier has set its sights on attaining market leadership in key product areas, and the company is confident it has the infrastructure in place to achieve those goals. The engineering team continues to develop fuel system solutions at a rapid pace with direct support from the parent company in Germany, led by majority owners and Co-CEOs, Markus and Andreas Gebhardt.

Technologically advanced products enabling Alfmeier's customers to meet

Alfmeier's modern facility in Greenville serves as a state-of-the-art headquarters and manufacturing base.

increasingly stringent EPA standards, combined with the company's strong plastic injection molding and manufacturing foundation, will secure Alfmeier's position as a leading supplier of automotive valving and fuel management systems in North America. The entire team at Alfmeier is committed to being the best in the industry and will continue to develop the solutions its customers require as part of its corporate mission. [■]

Alfmeier Corporation's management team is spearheaded by Executive Vice President for North America, Sam Konduros, and Co-Owner and CEO, Markus Gebhardt, of Germany.

World-class manufacturing practices in action at Alfmeier.

CONXUS™ Communications

A telecommunications revolution is underway, and CONXUS™ Communications, a narrowband personal communications services provider, is moving into a leadership position in the industry.

The privately held company is located in the heart of downtown Greenville at 12 North Main Street. It was founded by Cecil Duffie Jr., formerly CEO and co-founder of Dial Page, and Bill deKay, formerly COO of Dial Page. This experienced management team brought together senior executives from many of the nation's leading telecommunications companies. The expertise of the management team has resulted in CONXUS building a nationwide narrowband PCS network to deliver voice messaging services via Pocketalk™.

Since the company's inception in 1994, it has grown to more than 170 telecommunications professionals at the Greenville headquarters in addition to a substantial nationwide sales force.

Continuing the revitalization of downtown, CONXUS' new corporate headquarters are located at 12 North Main Street.

CONXUS began rolling out Pocketalk, known as "the answering machine for your pocket," to major markets across the country in the fall of 1997. The product combines the simplicity of voice messaging with the convenience of a portable answering machine to provide consumers both increased message content and freedom. Ideal for people on the go, Pocketalk receives complete private messages in the caller's own voice—eliminating the need to find a phone to call back and check messages. Moreover, this portability makes Pocketalk ideal for every situation where communications are important—whether for personal or business use.

CONXUS customers in the Washington DC/Baltimore and South Florida (Miami, Ft. Lauderdale, West Palm) markets have already purchased Pocketalk from the more than 300 distribution points during its initial launch. CONXUS has continued its successful introduction of Pocketalk to over 30,000 current customers in Tampa/St. Petersburg, Orlando, Dallas/Fort Worth, Houston, Los Angeles, Chicago, and Atlanta with several additional cities to launch in 1998. The technology will be available to Greenvillians sometime in 1999.

Prior to the introduction of Pocketalk, CONXUS conducted extensive research of the telecommunications market, confirming the enormous potential for the product. To meet the consumers demand for quality, CONXUS implemented a complex grid testing system in its markets, focusing on in-building coverage, speed of message delivery, and voice quality to assure Pocketalk would meet consumer expectations.

(left to right) Bill deKay, President of CONXUS; Cecil Duffie, CEO of CONXUS.

Pocketalk operates on a wireless network based on Motorola's InFLEXion protocol and voice messaging device, which allows high-speed transmission of voice messages and translates to reliable—and confirmed—voice message delivery.

CONXUS' next product Pocketext, the new data messaging device will be introduced in the third quarter of 1998 and will provide consumers enhanced text messaging services with guaranteed message delivery.

CONXUS was one of five companies awarded nationwide 50-kilohertz/50-kilohertz narrowband PCS licenses in 1994. The company augmented its capabilities for future growth by acquiring specialized mobile radio spectrum giving them an equivalent of a 175-kilohertz/175-kilohertz two-way network. In addition, the company is aggressively pursuing wholesale distribution for its network and pricing competitively which continues to enhance CONXUS' position in the marketplace.

Providing consumers the latest technology in the voice and data messaging market, accompanied by the best customer service in the industry positions CONXUS for many years of successful growth in its hometown, Greenville. ▣

207

BIC Corporation

BIC was founded in 1945 with the ingenuity and foresight of Marcel Bich, who started with very little and, in one generation, built his company into one of the most successful consumer products companies in the world.

At BIC, employees review the quality of writing instruments by using state-of-the-art, computer-automated write test machines.

Bich, who had been a production manager with a French ink manufacturer, purchased a factory outside Paris and went into business with his partner Edouard Buffard, as a maker of fountain pen parts and mechanical lead pencils.

In 1949, Bich introduced his version of the ballpoint pen in Europe, which he called, "BIC". He saw enormous potential for the product as long as it offered both quality and value. After experiencing much success in the European market, Bich entered the United States' market in 1958 by purchasing the Waterman Pen Company in Seymour, Connecticut.

Success followed in the United States and around the world as well. Today, BIC sells approximately 20 million writing instruments daily in 150 countries.

BIC Corporation, headquartered in Milford, Connecticut, is a subsidiary of Société BIC, located in Clichy, France. Société BIC S.A. operates BIC facilities worldwide and produces writing instruments, correction products, lighters, and shavers, as well as sailboards, under the name BIC Sport, and a line of designer clothing, under the name Guy Laroche.

In 1992, BIC entered the Greenville area by opening the doors to a facility in Fountain Inn. The company located much of its Research and Development Department for stationery products at the facility.

The Fountain Inn site was a logical choice for BIC. The Company was pleased with the close proximity to Greenville and its high concentration of engineers, strong educational system, and support from local and state government.

"At BIC, we always say that we win with people. The Company philosophy emphasizes the importance of giving responsibility to the individual, so that he, or she, can participate fully in the Company's growth and success," says Dr. Barry Chadwick, an area manager at the Fountain Inn facility.

"There is truly an entrepreneurial spirit throughout the BIC organization that is both challenging and rewarding at the same time," Chadwick says. "The BIC philosophy of empowerment and technical innovation, combined with Greenville's attractive lifestyle, make a great package to offer prospective employees."

Technology has also played a large role in the Company's success. BIC has always been, and will continue to be, a leader in the latest advancements in the industry. The Company uses state-of-the-art equipment in all stages of its manufacturing and testing processes. Constant quality control checks and rigorous testing of inks, points, correction fluids, tapes, and pens ensure that consumers get the very best stationery products on the market at a fair price.

Strengthening its position in the worldwide market has always been a priority for the Company. BIC carefully evaluates each and every acquisition it makes to ensure that any new addition is aligned with the company philosophy: providing maximum quality, value, and service at a fair price.

With more and more competitors entering the marketplace, BIC has taken an aggressive stance towards acquisitions over the past few years, purchasing Wite-Out® Products, Inc., a Beltsville, Maryland-based manufacturer of Wite-Out® correction fluids; Tipp-Ex®, Europe's leading manufacturer of correction products; Hauser®, a German manufacturer and distributor of writing instruments; and Sheaffer Pen Corporation, a Fort Madison, Iowa-based manufacturer with 80 years of experience in the premium writing instruments business.

Despite its recent entry in the local market, BIC has already established itself as a concerned corporate citizen that works for the betterment of the community. Its employees are active in organizations such as the United Way, the Greater Greenville Chamber of Commerce, and Junior Achievement. ⌐

The use of Microscopic Digital Imaging allows BIC employees to examine small parts for dimensional and surface properties.

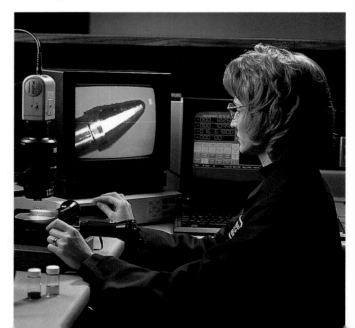

Marshall and Williams Company

Since its founding in 1920 in Providence, Rhode Island, Marshall and Williams Company has attained an impressive record of technical achievement while contributing significantly to the success of both the American textile industry and the plastic film industry.

The founders, Robert Marshall and John Williams, had as their original purpose the repair and service of tenter clips used by the New England textile finishing industry. Since that time the company has grown to design and build a broad spectrum of machinery for both the textile industry and the plastic film and sheet business.

In 1946, the company established its Southern operations in Greenville. They have now expanded to include the corporate headquarters and a large sheet metal fabrication facility on Airport Road, and Marshall and Williams Equipment Company on Highway 123 near Easley, in addition to the machinery manufacturing plant located on Pleasantburg Drive. These Greenville facilities comprise the Textile Division of the company with the Plastics Division remaining in Providence, Rhode Island.

Today, Marshall and Williams is a major textile industry leader in providing tentering and drying machinery for both woven and knitted fabrics of all types. Other types of equipment include industrial

ovens of various kinds, winding machinery, and electrical drives and control systems. Many of the machines developed by Marshall and Williams have been patented. "Since our beginning, the spirit of innovation has remained a constant driving force at Marshall and Williams," says Stuart MacDonald, President and CEO.

Besides providing high quality machinery and accessories to help keep textile companies competitive, Marshall and Williams also adds to its expertise by participating in the activities of several trade organizations. For many years, the company has been represented in the leadership of the American Textile Machinery Association, the Northern Textile Association, the American Association of Textile Chemists and Colorists, and several other trade groups.

The company's marketing efforts extend around the world, both by participation in the American Textile Machinery Exhibition-International (ATME-I), held

in Greenville, and in the international machinery show (ITMA) held in various countries in Europe. These efforts are supplemented by a network of sales agents in a number of foreign countries ranging from Central and South America to Africa to the Far East. This has resulted in Marshall and Williams having exported machinery to 40 countries circling the globe.

It is rare for a company in the American textile machinery industry to maintain the same good name and prosper for almost 80 years. Ongoing product innovation, unequaled customer service, and personnel stability have all contributed to this achievement. Marshall and Williams is proud to be a member of the Greenville business community and fully expects to be here for another 80 years.

209

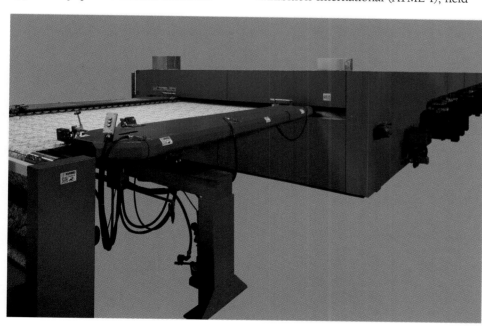

Precision Tool Manufacturer, Inc.

Through the tireless pursuit of quality and excellence, the eight person team at Precision Tool Manufacturer strives to ensure their customers return. They continually prove that the company is a top-notch manufacturing facility. This ensures

The principals of Precision Tool Manufacturer: (standing) Wendell Mattison, Executive Vice President/COO (seated) Merl F. Code, President/CEO.

that customers will not only repeat their business, but also tell others of Precision Tool Manufacturer's outstanding ability to perform above all the rest.

When Merl Code, owner and chief executive officer of Precision Tool Manufacturer, acquired the company in 1995, he saw an enormous amount of potential for the company on a local and global basis. The West Union based company, which has been in business since 1978, deals mainly in metal fabrication, primarily for the hydraulics industry, but is reaching into other specialty groups as well.

Code says he has lofty goals for Precision Tool Manufacturer and is confident that his employees are more than capable of accomplishing the job at hand. Since the acquisition, Code says the company has become a more efficient and cost-effective operation because of the hard work and dedication of the Precision Tool team.

Key points of achieving a lean operation according to Code are quality assurance and customer service. Producing products that meet client specifications—exactly—and delivering the order on time—every time—accentuates the true character of the Precision Tool team.

Everyone at Precision Tool Manufacturer takes an extreme amount of pride in their work, and the company's philosophy—"To produce the highest quality products, and deliver them to customers with an excellence of service that creates exceptional value and inspires customer confidence and loyalty"—outlines the company's promise to its customers.

To lead the Precision Tool team, Code hired Wendell Mattison, as executive vice president and chief operating officer, to oversee the everyday operations of the business. Mattison's background involves extensive management experience, which Code says he felt would best serve the company.

"We have made it a point to cross-train all of our employees, therefore we each know how to operate every piece of machinery at our facility so we never experience any down time," Mattison says. "Knowing as much as possible is the key, because we all know that if the company is successful, then we will be successful as well."

Precision Tool Manufacturer is a full service machine shop with capabilities ranging from high and low volume CNC machining, precision tooling, machines built to specifications, prototypes, and general machining to jigs and fixtures, turning and milling, assembly and/or sub-assembly, consulting, and designing.

"We make sure we're always listening to our customers, so we always meet their needs and exceed their expectations on every job that comes from our shop," Mattison says.

Precision tooling is much more than ensuring that every product is machined accurately to size within close limits. It is a business where a person's experience and expertise determine success. Precision Tool Manufacturer is a business in which project managers and craftsman are all trained and experienced in identifying individual product demands, then finding and implementing the most appropriate, efficient, and cost-effective solution. Precision Tool Manufacturer is committed corporately and individually to providing responsive, high quality services through employment of quality management practices.

Precision Tool Manufacturer has an impressive list of more than 20 valued customers. Included are four preferred clients who are Barker Air & Hydraulics; Pressure Devices, Inc.; Ross Controls; and Valenite, Inc. The Precision Tool team aspires the growth of their client list through hard work, skill, performance, and adaptability.

Precision Tool Manufacturer is pursuing the rating of ISO-9002, and certification is pending. Thus, the commitment of the Precision Tool team to its customers definitely makes it the company that is competent enough to promise and capable enough to deliver.

The quality of Precision Tool Manufacturer's products are out of this world.

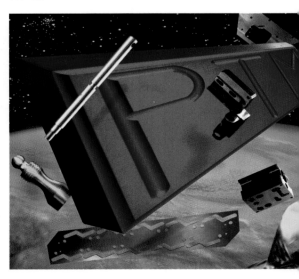

Steel Heddle

*T*hroughout its one hundred year history, if there's one word that best describes Steel Heddle's success, it's their ability to "adapt." Adapting to meet the textile industry's needs for weaving machine accessories is a way of life at Steel Heddle. After all, if your market in 1972 that was dependent on the 400,000 looms operating in USA mills, was now 95,000, you might wonder how Steel Heddle survived. Despite the smaller weaving machine population, those 95,000 machines turn out more fabric than the 400,000 due to higher speeds and wider widths.

Who is this 100 year old survivor, Steel Heddle? What are their products? And why have they prospered while most of the major USA textile machinery manufacturers have gone out of business?

Founded in Philadelphia, PA in 1898, Steel Heddle introduced the first "steel" heddle to America about the same time the first automatic loom was installed in a Vermont cotton mill. Faster loom speeds and improved fabric quality was a direct benefit from the new steel heddle. Today, Steel Heddle's products are used by thousands of textile mills throughout the world.

In the early twenties, Steel Heddle built its first manufacturing plant in Greenville, South Carolina. The first phase of the facility located on Rutherford Road, which is now headquarters, was built in 1948. Today this office and plant complex covers

Steel Heddle: Greenville, South Carolina.

475,000 square feet on 50 acres.

When weaving machine technology shifted outside the USA in the early '60s, textile mills in America had no choice but to buy weaving machines from Europe and the Far East. Steel Heddle changed their products to provide American mills weaving machine accessories compatible with every make and model loom on the market. This meant customers still enjoyed the advantages of local support, faster service, and lower cost.

Another historical decision was when Steel Heddle began manufacturing its own special steel wire used in heddles, drop wires, and reeds. Steel Heddle's Westminster, South Carolina steel plant is a showcase of state-of-the-art equipment. Here, proprietary processes roll and temper wire in an exclusive environment. Today, a large part of the Westminster wire production goes to customers in the aerospace, electronics, automotive, and electrical industries where precise tolerances and special packaging are critical.

One Hundred Years Strong

The products of Steel Heddle. All weaving machines are fitted with four key components that, working in unison, control the pattern or style of the fabric to

Steel Heddle: Westminster, South Carolina.

be woven. They are: Heddles, Harness Frames, Reeds, and Drop Wires. Without them, the complex art of weaving fabric would not be possible. Steel Heddle is the only company in the world that manufactures all four accessories and the only heddle and frame manufacturer in the United States.

Technology at work. Higher and higher loom speeds provide the greatest challenge to the company's products. Today, high speed air jet weaving machines reach speeds of 1200 ppm. A totally vertical operation, Steel Heddle will develop its own tools when machines on the market are not capable of meeting their quality requirements. In 1989, Steel Heddle inaugurated its company-wide Quality Assurance Program. The company has received ISO Certification and continues to receive quality awards from customers. From the beginning, commitment to product innovation, exclusive patented products and designs, and a dedication to the textile industry that their customers can measure in productivity and quality gains have earned Steel Heddle the right to claim, "we're your partner in the weave room." This is no idle claim. The fact that at least 85-90 percent of the weaving mills in the U.S. have part of their accessory package supplied by Steel Heddle certainly bears that out.

211

Schweizerhall Development Company & Schweizerhall Manufacturing

In response to the significant outsourcing trend in the pharma and fine chemicals markets, Schweizerhall Development Company opened a new development laboratory in Greenville in early 1997. The local facility increased Schweizerhall's chemical capabilities threefold over the previous lab in South Plainfield, New Jersey.

To further meet industry needs, Schweizerhall Manufacturing Company came on line in mid-1998 with a commercial scale manufacturing plant. This facility, which contains vessels from a 200 to 2,000 gallon capacity in both glass and stainless steel, affords Schweizerhall the ability to provide intermediates and drug substances from multi-gram to multi-ton quantities at one site.

The development and manufacturing companies both operate under the corporate umbrella of Schweizerhall, Inc., in Piscataway, New Jersey. The parent company, Schweizerhall Holding Group, is based in Switzerland and was founded in the early 1900s for manufacturing salts and dyes for the textile industry. The company then developed a worldwide distribution system and expanded into commodity chemicals. In 1988, Schweizerhall acquired the U.S. firm, Chemical Dynamics, and expanded through investment and business increases in sales and markets for pharmaceuticals,

Schweizerhall Development Company, opened in early 1997, is located on Perimeter Road in Greenville, South Carolina.

specialty chemicals, and value-added chemical products.

Through a close working relationship with a team of technical and sales colleagues at Schweizerhall's corporate headquarters, the Greenville development facility operates a reactor laboratory. In addition, the development facility includes organic laboratories, an analytical lab, chemists offices, service areas for glassware washrooms, dryer room for vacuum tray dryers, chemical storerooms, as well as conference rooms, administrative support offices, and a library. All labs at the facility are designed to perform synthetic organic chemistry as well as research chemistry under full GMP (Good Manufacturing Practices).

The chemists and laboratories of Schweizerhall are equipped to develop commercially viable and validatable processes for specialty chemicals in the areas of pharmaceuticals, flavor and fragrances, diagnostics, and other value-added chemicals. Most importantly, the chemists of Schweizerhall are constantly striving to find safer and more efficient methods for developing these specialty and fine chemicals. To ensure quality, an analytical services group develops analytical methods for testing the identity and purity of the organic chemical intermediates and products coming from the process development group.

As a responsible corporate citizen, Schweizerhall works under GMP guidelines, which assure a high-quality product with excellent documentation and operating procedures. Also, keeping within the spirit of GMP, Schweizerhall prides itself in working pro-actively with the FDA, EPA, and other regulatory agencies.

Through the continuous efforts Schweizerhall makes to ensure quality and comply with federal regulations, customers can rest assured Schweizerhall is

Schweizerhall Manufacturing Company (under construction at press time) was opened in mid-1998 to further meet industry needs.

there to provide unmatched customer service. Schweizerhall works on a contract basis for a variety of customers, most of which are pharmaceutical firms.

Due to the pro-business environment and quality business associates nearby, Schweizerhall, Inc. chose Donaldson Center as the site to locate its development laboratory and its manufacturing plant. Greenville's strong economy, skilled labor force, and solid infrastructure weighed heavily on the company's decision.

The future for Schweizerhall in South Carolina looks bright, indeed. In the coming years, the company will place more focus on pharmaceutical products and work to engage in long-term business relationships with branded pharmaceutical firms and emerging industries. Schweizerhall's presence in Greenville will have a significant economic impact on the community as well. The company intends to hire all engineers, contractors, construction workers, and consultants on a local basis to assist with future expansions.

Caterpillar

*C*aterpillar Inc. is the world's largest manufacturer of construction and mining equipment, diesel and natural gas engines, and industrial gas turbines. The company manufactures 75 percent of its products in the United States, but half of the company's sales are to customers outside the United States.

The company recorded 1997 sales of $19 billion and expects to grow to a $30 billion company in the next decade. Caterpillar products are manufactured in more than 70 locations around the world and employs more than 65,000 people.

As a Fortune 50 industrial company, Caterpillar has been named by *Fortune* magazine as one of the "World's Most Admired Companies" along with other great corporations like Coca-Cola, British Airways, and Toyota Motor Co."

The predecessors of Caterpillar began in the fields of California in the late 1800s. To harvest large crops of grain, farmers used "Combined Harvesters" which were pulled by as many as 40 horses. One combine builder, Benjamin Holt, recognized the need for more power and began building combines powered by steam engines. These "steamers" were huge, hard to handle, and often required a large crew of men to operate them. They were driven by large wheels and often became stuck in soft soil. Holt eventually

Caterpillar 3126 Marine Propulsion Engine.

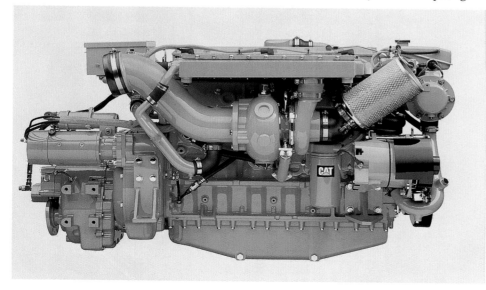

solved the floatation problem by developing and producing the first practical track-type tractor. It was first operated near Stockton, California on November 24, 1904.

Although Holt began using the trademark "Caterpillar" around that time, he didn't register it as a trademark until 1910. In 1906, Holt built his first experimental gasoline-powered Crawler Tractor, which was used to build the Los Angeles Aqueduct. At one time, there were over 100 Holt machines in operation in the Mojave Desert. In 1909, Holt expanded eastward and began building gasoline-powered Crawler Tractors in East Peoria, Illinois. In 1925, Caterpillar Tractor Company was formed by the merger of C.L. Best Tractor Company (another California Company) and Holt Manufacturing. Caterpillar Tractor Company showed a profit each year throughout the Great Depression except 1932. It was also during this time that Caterpillar Tractor Company began building diesel engines to power its tractors.

From this rather humble beginning, Caterpillar expanded and has become a large, multinational corporation. Much of that expansion occurred after World War II, when Caterpillar still had only two plants, one at East Peoria and the other at San Leandro, California. Today, Caterpillar is headquartered in Peoria, Illinois and is one of only a handful of U.S. companies that leads its industry while competing

globally from a principally domestic manufacturing base.

Long recognized as a world class manufacturer of engines and heavy industrial equipment, Caterpillar located an engine facility in Fountain Inn's Southchase Industrial Park in 1994.

Engines, such as the 3126B model, are assembled at the local facility for marine applications, recreational vehicles, industrial equipment, and for shipment to other plants. Truck engines are also produced at the Greenville facility. This location has proven to be ideal for this market, allowing quick delivery to many truck manufacturers.

Since Caterpillar's arrival in South Carolina, the state has proven to be a gracious host. Just as Caterpillar's Greenville plant opened, the company received an order for more than 2,000 of its 3100 series engines. The customer was the state, which purchased the engines for installation in a new fleet of school buses. The cooperation between the state, the school bus manufacturer, and Caterpillar illustrates a unique partnering between industry and local government.

Caterpillar's Greenville facility is doing its part to foster strong ties with area residents as well. Caterpillar is committed to the Greenville community and supports a number of education and civic affairs such as United Way, March of Dimes, YMCA, and others. Caterpillar also encourages its employees to maintain an active role in becoming more involved with the community as well. ⌐

213

16

Chapter Sixteen

Professions

Day & Zimmermann, Inc.

Pride in the past and commitment to the future is the driving force behind Day & Zimmermann, Inc. Founded in 1901 by Charles Day, an electrical engineer, and Kern Dodge, a mechanical engineer, the company focused on helping industry improve its operating efficiency by "modernizing" engineering.

Both men pioneered the application of electric motors to replace belt drives on machine tools. Early customers of this application were Link-Belt Engineering Company (1901), Jeansville Iron Works (1902), Westinghouse Electric & Manufacturing Company (1903), and Victor Talking Machine Company (1904). Soon thereafter, Day's friend and classmate, John Zimmermann, joined the partnership, and the company has been growing ever since.

Responding to the evolving needs of its clients, Day & Zimmermann adopted and operates under a code of values to provide a safe work environment and continuous opportunity for employees, operate with integrity, provide quality products and services, make a profit, create a family atmosphere, and support the communities in which the company functions. Today's leaders of Day & Zimmermann remain committed to these same operational values.

As Day & Zimmermann approaches its

Three Day & Zimmermann companies reside at the Piedmont Center.

centennial anniversary, the company remains a private firm that has grown to one of the world's largest and most diversified privately held professional services firms, with approximately 14,000 employees. The company operates from more than 140 locations worldwide and has completed projects in over 75 countries. The company's headquarters is located in Philadelphia.

Notable projects the company has been involved with throughout the years include designing the foil wrapping machines in 1914 for Hershey Kisses and designing and managing the construction of 3M Company's expansion in Greenville from the Philadelphia offices in 1975. Ironically, Greenville was chosen as a site where Day & Zimmermann would later locate a business unit and continue its strong relationship with 3M.

In 1992, Day & Zimmermann's Greenville operation was established because of the company's interest in expanding in the industrial market of the Southeast. Long recognized as an engineering center with ample resources, Greenville made good business sense as a location for expansion. One of the deciding factors at the time was the interest of several people with long histories at other engineering companies in the area to build a strong engineering group and, in turn, to support the industrial market. The office was built on the work ethic

Harold L. Yoh, Jr., Chairman & CEO.

behind the corporate motto of "We Do What We Say."

The Greenville operation's initial focus was on providing engineering services through Day & Zimmermann International. Since then, additional business units of the company have joined the local operation. Services have been expanded to include full-service operations and facilities' management through Day & Zimmermann Services as well as design/build contracting through Day & Zimmermann Construction.

Day & Zimmermann International provides engineering, procurement, and construction services to its clients both domestically and internationally. The Greenville office, one of three Southeast operation centers, focuses on markets such as fibers, film, tobacco, glass, specialty chemicals, and general manufacturing. Day & Zimmermann International's strength is its capability to manage an entire engineering and construction effort, from concept to plant start-up and production.

Day & Zimmermann Services (DZS) specializes in providing operation and maintenance services for government installations and federal/municipal buildings. DZS projects range from total

3M at Donaldson Center—one of Day & Zimmermann's many clients.

the area's stature as an international commercial center.

The company will also continue to help industrial clients become more profitable by improving their operations. As the Day & Zimmermann staff grows, the employees will be more active as members of the community by supporting area businesses and contributing to the overall quality of life. With so many lifelong Greenvillians on staff and many others who now call this area home, it's no surprise Day & Zimmermann is committed to Greenville. ⌐⌐

infrastructure operation and maintenance services to military family housing maintenance and repair for over 7,000 Navy and Army housing units including the Naval Weapons Station in Charleston, South Carolina and Fort Bragg, North Carolina.

Following in the footsteps of Day & Zimmermann's founders, today's employees share the goal of helping the company's clients make their operations more efficient and profitable. Their resulting success enables them to invest money back into the community through employment opportunities and local purchasing practices. Also, the company's direct hire construction group, Day & Zimmermann Construction, has a standard policy of hiring local labor and specialty contractors whenever possible, rather than importing them from another region.

In addition to its operating philosophy and the tremendous increase in outsourcing by client companies, Day & Zimmermann attributes much of its modern day success to an expanded range of services and the high demand for process controls and systems integration.

Day & Zimmermann has been owned by the Yoh family of Pennsylvania since 1961. Family values, closeness, and balance between professional and home life are some of the guiding principles that set this company apart from much of its competition. The Yohs have formally adopted a set of family values, some of which overlap with the company's values.

Safety, quality, and integrity are the company's first three corporate values of great importance to the Yohs, as are family and community. The local office ran a televised public service announcement on traffic safety during the '97-98 holiday season in support of its first corporate value, "Safety." The office was presented an award by the National Highway Traffic Safety Administration/Department of Transportation for the safety announcement.

Employees and their families are entrenched in the community and are deeply committed to it. They enjoy the quality of life in Greenville, and many of the 160 local employees are life-long Greenvillians. Employees at all levels are active in local civic organizations. Day & Zimmermann supports the Special Olympics, Hospice, Junior Achievement, United Way, Little League Baseball, and Boys Home of the South, among others. Some staff members serve as leaders in local chapters of national professional associations such as the Project Management Institute, Construction Industry Institute, Building Owners and Managers Association (BOMA), and the Institute of Electrical and Electronics Engineers.

As the Greenville area continues on its fast track of growth and development, Day & Zimmermann will be there. The company intends to expand and diversify by adding business units to complement

"Cajun Crawfish Boil"—annual event enjoyed by Day & Zimmermann employees and families.

Gibbes, Gallivan, White & Boyd, P.A.

From its inception in 1948 to its present size of 30 attorneys and 40 support staff members, the law firm of Gibbes, Gallivan, White & Boyd, P.A. has grown and adapted to meet the ever-changing needs of its clients in South Carolina and the Southeast. The firm's offices have been located at 330 East Coffee Street since 1984, convenient to both the Clement F. Haynsworth, Jr. Federal Building and the newly renovated Greenville County Courthouse.

The firm offers a variety of legal services. Its attorneys represent clients in both state and federal courts, and before administrative and regulatory agencies. Its attorneys are admitted to practice in South Carolina, North Carolina, Georgia, Florida, Tennessee, Pennsylvania, Massachusetts, and Colorado.

Gibbes, Gallivan, White & Boyd, P.A. takes an aggressive approach to client service by emphasizing not only the management and conclusion of litigation, but also the importance of advice and counseling to assist clients in avoiding

Attorneys are actively involved in serving the community through organizations such as the Senior Action Center.

unnecessary litigation. In an effort to provide the most current legal and professional advice, the firm regularly presents seminars to both its individual clients and the business community. The firm strives to aid its clients to prevent legal problems. The firm's attorneys have assisted in the development of safety programs, drafted handbooks and manuals, conducted audits to assure compliance with current laws, established quality assurance programs, and written numerous articles on emerging legal issues.

The firm's clients include some of the largest publicly traded and privately held companies, as well as banks, railroads, governmental entities, professional associations, small businesses, and major insurance companies. The firm's areas of practice include banking, commercial real estate and development, corporate and business transactions, bankruptcy, products liability, general litigation, insurance defense and coverage litigation, labor and employment law, workers' compensation, toxic tort litigation, environmental law, design and construction law, and civil rights litigation. The attorneys of the firm are among the most experienced and

The firm's offices are located in the Central Business District at 330 East Coffee Street.

respected litigators and counselors as well as being skilled in alternative dispute resolution measures such as mediation and arbitration.

In an effort to meet the needs of this diverse client base, the firm has adopted a team approach to litigation management, dividing specialized practice areas into teams of attorneys led by a partner and staffed by attorneys and paralegals. Using this team approach, the firm can consistently provide clients with excellent legal services in an efficient and cost effective manner.

The firm has also capitalized on the latest available technologies to further enhance quality and efficiency. The firm has installed a new, state-of-the-art computer network with internet access. The firm has also supplemented its extensive legal library with the latest CD-ROM capabilities accessible directly from the desk of each attorney. The firm also uses computer assisted legal research which allows access to legal resources across the country, and to a host of other data and information resources.

Gibbes, Gallivan, White & Boyd, P.A. is committed to serving not only its clients but also the local community. Its attorneys actively participate in many civic and community service organizations.

Attorneys from the firm have held leadership positions in numerous community and charitable organizations such as the Junior League of Greenville; Prevent Child Abuse Carolina; Mental Health Association; Greenville Civic Ballet; Rotary; Sertoma; Kiwanis; Greenville Literacy Association; Speech, Hearing, and Learning Center; Metropolitan Arts Council; St. Francis Hospital Foundation; Greenville Zoo; Senior Action Center; and many others.

Firm attorneys are also active in the city's many downtown festivals, such as Fall for Greenville and the Riverplace Festival. The firm's attorneys actively support the United Way of Greenville County through service on its board and committees and support of its Loaned Executive and Palmetto Society programs. Firm members also actively participate in local business organizations such as the Chamber of Commerce, and the firm has had nine graduates of Leadership Greenville and one graduate of Leadership Spartanburg.

The attorneys of Gibbes, Gallivan, White & Boyd, P.A. are actively involved in professional legal organizations and have served in leadership roles on the boards and committees of the South Carolina Bar, the Greenville County Bar, and the South Carolina Defense Trial Attorneys' Association. Its attorneys are also actively involved in the Defense Research Institute, Federation of Insurance and Corporate Counsel, Trial Attorneys of America, National Association of Railroad Trial Counsel, and American Bar Association.

The law firm of Gibbes, Gallivan, White & Boyd, P.A. continues to be actively involved in all aspects of the Greenville community. Whether providing clients with the utmost professional experience, aiding in new community developments, participating in charitable organizations, or supporting any of the numerous community campaigns, the lawyers of Gibbes, Gallivan, White & Boyd, P.A. practice much more than law—they practice consistent support of the growth and enrichment of Greenville and the surrounding area. ◖

Nelson Mullins Riley & Scarborough, L.L.P.

For more than 100 years, the law firm of Nelson Mullins Riley & Scarborough, L.L.P., or "Nelson Mullins," has been firmly woven into the fabric of South Carolina with strong ties in the Upstate.

Nelson Mullins is a full service law firm with six offices in South Carolina, North Carolina, and Georgia. The firm, founded in 1897 in Columbia, South Carolina, currently has more than 200 lawyers. Nelson Mullins is the largest law firm in South Carolina, with four offices

The firm's enhanced computer technology links the firm's six offices in North Carolina, South Carolina, and Georgia.

and more than 140 lawyers throughout the state.

As a regional law firm with strong roots in the business community and an appreciation for new directions in management, Nelson Mullins is constantly adapting to its clients' diverse and changing needs. Services offered by the firm include start-up assistance for growth companies and international investments, complex multi-party litigation, and representation of regional underwriters and investment bankers in financial areas. The Greenville office of Nelson Mullins also has expertise in corporate, securities, tax, labor and

employment, immigration, complex shareholder disputes, mergers and acquisitions, and commercial and product liability litigation. Many of the firm's clients, including growth companies, expanding local businesses, and major international companies headquartered in the Southeast, look to the firm for all of their legal services.

A Tradition of Leadership

The firm opened its Greenville office in 1987 when former South Carolina Governor Richard W. Riley, his father E.P. "Ted" Riley, and his brother E.P. Riley Jr., joined the firm. Dick Riley, a Greenville native and Furman University graduate, left the firm in 1993 to become United States Secretary of Education. By 1998 the Greenville office had become one of the Upstate's largest full service law firms under the leadership of several individuals, including John Campbell, Jr., Kenneth Young, Robert Erwin, Sheryl Blenis Ortmann, Marvin Quattlebaum, Walter Tollison, Steven Wynkoop, Erroll Anne Hodges, David Hodge, Henry Burwell, Russell Plowden, Walter Hinton, Kym Mahnke, and William Brown.

Leadership positions held by partners in the firm include the Board of Governors and House of Delegates of the American Bar Association and the South Carolina Bar, President of the Defense Research Institute, the South Carolina Defense Trial Attorney's Association, Lawyers for Civil Justice, and the South Carolina Bar. The firm's attorneys are frequent lecturers at legal education programs and enjoy working with many Upstate civic organizations and charities. The firm has been a major contributor to the Peace Center, the South Carolina Children's Theatre, the Richard W. Riley Math and Science Building at Furman University, the Greenville Symphony, and the Thornblade Classic, among others. In 1998 and 1999, the Greenville office of Nelson Mullins will fund a fellowship for a first-year attorney to work for the Legal Services Agency of Western Carolina and to focus exclusively on cases which effect children.

The Poinsett Plaza on Main Street will be the new home of the Greenville office of Nelson Mullins in 1999.

National Reputation

Nelson Mullins has acquired a national reputation for tort defense, product liability, commercial, environmental, and software litigation. The firm's attorneys have represented clients nationally in matters involving product liability claims in industries as diverse as chemicals, asbestos, pharmaceuticals, automobile and truck manufacturers, and other manufacturing processes. The firm's environmental and toxic tort attorneys represent industrial and commercial clients ranging from complex, multi-party litigation to civil and criminal enforcement. Attorneys in the business litigation area advise clients on such matters as class action suits, contract disputes, corporate takeovers, professional liability, securities, financial fraud, and civil and criminal tax audits by the Internal Revenue Service and the South Carolina Department of Revenue.

Each of the firm's offices offers a unique combination of business specialties and expertise. For example, the Atlanta and Charlotte offices have substantial experience in the representation of computer and technology businesses, banks and financial institutions, health care organizations, investment banks, and transportation companies. The four South Carolina offices have worked in concert to assist with a number of recent major

investments and the construction of new plants by foreign companies in the State of South Carolina, including BMW in the Upstate and Mikasa in Charleston. The Greenville office is one of the largest full

service law firms in the Upstate and is uniquely distinctive in its ability to call in expertise, as needed, from the firm's Atlanta, Charlotte, and other South Carolina offices.

Committed To Greenville

The Greenville office of Nelson Mullins has had a significant impact on the firm's past and present and will play an important role in its future. Because of the firm's unique location along the I-85 corridor and the support from its offices in other major southeastern cities, Nelson Mullins is uniquely positioned to provide all aspects of legal representation for its clients, large and small. ◖

Ken Young and Kym Mahnke are proud of Nelson Mullins' contributions and commitment to the South Carolina Children's Theatre.

Haynsworth, Marion, McKay & Guérard, L.L.P.

*L*eadership is a characteristic inherent to those who practice law. Whether it's examining the status quo, instituting change, ensuring the community's continued growth, or safeguarding the progress of their predecessors, the attorneys of Haynsworth, Marion, McKay & Guérard, L.L.P. have taken the lead in the Greenville community for well over a century.

The attorneys at Haynsworth, Marion, McKay & Guérard, L.L.P. have a passion for their work, thus making their careers an avocation as opposed to just a vocation.

Integrity, Professionalism and Client Service

Since its inception in 1882, the firm has held to the tradition of personal integrity, professionalism, and client service established by its founder, H.J. Haynsworth. His son, Clement Furman Haynsworth, who joined the firm in 1905, maintained his father's standards of excellence.

During the early 1920s, the firm's growth was tied to the expanding local textile industry. Even before the Upstate became known as the textile capital of the world, the Haynsworth firm provided counsel to textile manufacturers in the emerging commercial center of the Upstate. Throughout its history, the firm has continued to build on this legacy of experience and participation in the growth of the Upstate community.

Haynsworth, Marion, McKay & Guérard's attorneys fondly recall the firm's history of leaders: one early partner, Miss James Perry, was a true pioneer. The first woman admitted to the bar of South Carolina, "Miss Jim" served as a tax specialist and provided counsel to a number of corporate clients. Through the years, the firm's prominent attorneys have enhanced the scope of the practice and provided meaningful leadership to the Upstate and the profession.

Meeting Today's Challenges

Haynsworth, Marion, McKay & Guérard, L.L.P. is a comprehensive state-wide civil practice involved in virtually all

Partners of Haynsworth, Marion, McKay & Guérard, L.L.P.: (left to right) Knox H. White, Anne S. Ellefson, Brent O. E. Clinkscale, and G. Dewey Oxner, Jr.

areas of state and federal law. The firm's areas of legal specialization include business transactions, municipal finance, securities, health care, employment, taxation, estate planning and administration, employer benefits, real estate, bankruptcy, and workers' compensation. The firm also specializes in the litigation areas of professional malpractice, environmental, medical device and product liability, and construction litigation.

Most recently, the firm expanded its services within its Governmental Law Department to include the representation of international companies affected by state and local legislation in South Carolina. With the state being an acknowledged leader in attracting international investments, Haynsworth has assisted clients with matters related to economic incentives for new and expanding industries, U.S. Customs Service issues, NAFTA, import quotas, foreign outsourcing, and immigration.

Both professionally and personally, partners and associates at Haynsworth, Marion, McKay & Guérard, L.L.P. meet the challenges of representing business and governmental clients at every opportunity as the state becomes a major center of commerce in the Southeast.

Many of today's most pressing issues are

routine challenges at the firm. The firm has been involved in major initiatives in the Upstate including the financing of the BI-LO Center, creation of the Greenville County Infrastructure Bond Bank, and structuring major healthcare projects. Haynsworth attorneys are often called upon to serve in leadership positions on governmental and community boards in furtherance of the development of the Upstate.

Since the firm's beginning, it has been dedicated to the future of the state, and the firm will remain committed throughout the years to come. ◖◗

Jeff Dezen Public Relations (JDPR)

Imagine a leading sporting goods client asking for ideas to sell a half-million dozen golf balls to clear the way for the introduction of a new ball line. Or a manufacturing company with an identity crisis hoping to redefine itself via a new name and overhauled image. Importantly, neither business was interested in the expense of an advertising campaign but, rather, believed that smart public relations strategies could deliver.

When Dunlop Maxfli Sports Corporation asked Jeff Dezen Public Relations (JDPR) to develop a strategy to sell its remaining quantities of the discontinued lines of Maxfli MD and HT golf balls, the PR firm was up to the task. Crafting a campaign called "Tee Up and Take Off," Maxfli and the JDPR team joined with Delta Airlines, offering a free companion ticket to purchasers of a dozen

JDPR's newly renovated 100-year-old office building combines historic preservation with contemporary accents—a perfect 'home' for this dynamic agency, in the heart of the city's downtown district, at 13-A East Coffee Street.

Maxfli balls. The promotion's popularity—driven by aggressive media relations tactics—spread nationwide, being featured on "Oprah," CNN, and in national travel and sports publications, as well as in daily newspapers.

The result: market share for the MD ball line increased more than 500 percent and the HT ball line more than 70 percent, pushing Maxfli past its closest competitor in total golf ball sales.

When BK Industries (BKI), formerly the Barbecue King Company, approached JDPR about launching a corporate restage, JDPR developed a comprehensive strategy for the job at hand. The challenge was to create and introduce a new corporate identity and portray the new BKI as a progressive foodservice equipment manufacturer—a leader through innovation—while at the same time leveraging the company's rich heritage in the foodservice industry.

From strategic positioning to logo remake, trade show splashes to direct-mail pieces, and more, BKI's management team and JDPR were able to successfully launch the new corporate identity as well as introduce new products through sustaining sequential campaign efforts.

BKI's restage yielded record-breaking sales, immediate market-response to its new "flagship" product, and unprecedented industry attention to innovative communications materials reflecting the company's new image. The year-and-a-half long campaign culminated in BKI's being named Manufacturer of the Year in 1997 by one of the industry's most prestigious trade associations.

Whether a client's needs include a new product launch, a nationwide media relations campaign, comprehensive trade show coordination, or any other number of public relations tasks, the JDPR team always strives to exceed client expectations . . . starting with deliberate strategic planning, clearly defining goals and objectives, and excelling in follow-through.

The JDPR team brings an impressive list of credentials to the table. With backgrounds in sports marketing, not-for-profit

Creative idea generation is at the core of the PR firm's capabilities. Client work highlights the company's conference room (pictured) and is proudly displayed throughout JDPR's office setting.

work, print journalism, and sports broadcasting, the public relations professionals at JDPR have a wealth of knowledge and experience to share with its growing list of valued clients.

JDPR specializes in putting its talents to work for its clients. However, those talents came in handy as JDPR staged a widely publicized move of its own in 1997. The company now occupies a one-hundred-year-old office building at 13-A East Coffee Street in the heart of downtown Greenville. The agency took great care to keep the building's historical character intact while blending a contemporary look to match the agency's dynamic and energetic spirit, which has established it as one of the premier public relations agencies in the Southeast. **◥**

Ogletree, Deakins, Nash, Smoak & Stewart, P.C.

When companies from Maine to Florida or the Carolinas to California look for a firm to handle important labor and employment matters, they often select Ogletree, Deakins, Nash, Smoak & Stewart, a firm that was founded 21 years ago with 16 lawyers and offices in Greenville and Atlanta. This continued selection by companies across the country has resulted in the addition of nine offices and the hiring of more than 100 additional attorneys.

Greenville-Based But Nationally Recognized

The firm's practice is both local, representing 19 of the Upstate's 25 largest manufacturing plants, as well as national, with 31 of the *Fortune 50* calling on the firm to assist in solving important legal matters. The firm's clients range from local companies employing only a handful of people to airlines with hundreds of locations and tens of thousands of employees. From auto manufacturing to telecommunications, banks to petroleum refineries, and construction and chemicals to papermaking, Ogletree clients include leading companies in all U.S. business segments.

The firm has continued its employment and environmental law specialties but has also added construction law and litigation in a variety of fields. These areas have grown dramatically in recent years. In 1998, 14 of the firm's lawyers were listed in the prestigious publication *The Best Lawyers in America.*

Rather than diversify into additional practice areas, the firm's growth instead has been in representing clients on a broad geographic scale, recently handling matters in 49 states. The Greenville office has provided initial staffing for offices in Raleigh, Nashville, Columbia, and Charleston. During 1996 and 1997 respectively, entire labor and employment practices of general practice firms joined Ogletree and constitute the firm's Houston and Birmingham offices. In January 1999, Ogletree will merge with an established labor and employment firm in Chicago.

The firm's reputation was initially built on the high profile union organizing campaigns of the '70s and '80s. The employment practice has rapidly expanded to encompass all aspects of the labor and employment area as it has changed to reflect the global economy and the plethora of new laws designed to provide

additional rights to employees. For example, the firm recently added a multilingual lawyer as the sixth attorney in its immigration practice. As employee benefits has changed to a more regulated specialty, the firm has expanded its benefits practice to include five tax lawyers, many of whom have advanced degrees and/or CPA designations. The firm will continue to add expertise in each of its practice areas as required to serve its clients.

The environmental practice group handles all types of enforcement actions, permitting, litigation, regulatory review and auditing, and includes lawyers with over 25 years of specialization in environmental matters.

The firm's construction practice represents owners, general contractors, and sureties throughout the southeast in contract development, negotiations, arbitrations, mediation, and litigation. These attorneys have extensive experience in handling complex construction and surety issues.

Despite vigorous travel and practice schedules, the firm's lawyers devote considerable time to community activities, serving in leadership positions in organizations such as the Chamber of Commerce, Donaldson Center Air Park, Goodwill Industries, Urban League, American Cancer Society, Greenville Symphony, and United Way. ▣

Greenville Shareholders Standing:
Phillip L. Conner, Robert O. King,
L. Gray Geddie Jr., Fred W. Suggs Jr.,
Phillip A. Kilgore, John W. Hoag III,
Ralph M. Mellom, Kimila L. Wooten,
Donald A. Cockrill, Ingrid Blackwelder
Erwin, M. Baker Wyche III, E. Grantland
Burns, Lewis T. Smoak, Joel A. Daniel,
J. Hamilton Stewart III. Front Row:
L. Franklin Elmore, Glenn R. Goodwin,
Kristofer K. Strasser, G. Scott Humphrey,
Ronald E. Cardwell, Mark M. Stubley.
Not pictured: R. Allison Phinney,
Mary Lou Hill, Nancy W. Monts.

Locations in: Atlanta, Birmingham,
Charleston, Chicago, Columbia,
Greenville, Houston, Nashville, Raleigh,
Washington, and Winston-Salem.

Jacobs Engineering Group Inc.

Greenvillians have long recognized Sirrine as a provider of high-quality engineering and construction services to a diversified portfolio of clients around the globe. This reputation for excellence developed well beyond Greenville and throughout the engineering and construction industry, prompting Pasadena-based Jacobs Engineering Group to acquire Sirrine from CRSS in 1994.

Core Values Drive Jacobs' Direction

Jacobs' evolution into a global company has been guided by the same values followed by founder Dr. Joseph J. Jacobs when he began the company over 50 years ago. As the 21st century approaches, Jacobs unifies its employees with three core values: it is a relationship-based company; people are its greatest asset; and growth is an imperative. These values embrace national and cultural differences while driving its business forward with a common vision—to be the best and the safest engineering and construction company in the world.

Jacobs receives over 90 percent of its business from repeat clients, reflecting the company's preference for clients who conduct their business in a long-term, relationship-based manner. Jacobs earns this client loyalty by continually striving to surpass client expectations on each and every project.

Jacobs provided construction services for a major expansion of BMW's manufacturing facility here in Upstate South Carolina.

As a professional services company, the value Jacobs provides to its clients originates entirely from the collective contributions of its employees. The company delivers its services in a team environment—making team-building skills a critical prerequisite with its clients. Jacobs' training programs and operational practices acknowledge these important skills, and place equal importance on personal and interpersonal levels of development.

Prospering in a competitive marketplace demands growth. To sustain steady, profitable growth Jacobs concentrates on what it does best—engineering and construction. Such growth creates loyal shareholders, delighted clients, and satisfied employees.

Geographic and Market Diversification

Today, with its Southern Region headquarters located in Greenville, South Carolina, Jacobs has grown into one of the largest engineering and construction companies in the U.S. Over 18,000 employees in 35 major full-service offices located domestically and overseas perform thousands of projects annually. Jacobs offers its services across multiple lines of business including chemicals and polymers; pharmaceuticals and biotechnologies; buildings and infrastructure; basic resources; federal programs; pulp and paper; semiconductor; petroleum; and consumer products and durables. With annual revenues from these lines of business nearing $2 billion, Jacobs is widely regarded as one of the best-managed

Jacobs provided engineering and construction services for Chevron's $300 million refinery modernization project in Richmond, California.

companies in the engineering and construction industry.

In addition to providing engineering services, the Greenville office provides architectural, procurement, construction, and maintenance services, and serves as a window to Jacobs' worldwide resources. This office focuses primarily on the pulp and paper, chemical, and manufacturing industries, but can serve nearly any industry by mobilizing unique talents and resources through the company's virtual office network. These global electronic links encourage standardization of operating procedures, giving Jacobs' clients the same high standard of service regardless of location.

Clear Path Into the Future

Jacobs has a clear path forward—focus on its core business, unite its employees through common values and work practices, and maximize client delight through exceptional project execution. By doing this, Jacobs will continue laying groundwork for broader opportunities and fresh challenges into the 21st century. ▣

Wyche, Burgess, Freeman & Parham, P.A.

Clients of Wyche, Burgess, Freeman & Parham, P.A. have the benefit of working with highly skilled lawyers who have been trained at the nation's leading law schools and who are seasoned professional problem-solvers with an extensive knowledge of community and statewide issues.

The firm has played an important role in the creation and expansion of a number of Greenville's major corporations—a large diversified media organization, the nation's leading manufacturer of electronic capacitors, South Carolina's largest commercial bank, and a fully-integrated textile company. In fact, the firm's general counsel representation includes nearly half of the publicly-traded corporations headquartered in Greenville, in addition to numerous privately held businesses, large and small.

Practice areas offered by the firm include corporate finance, securities, taxation, civil litigation, trade secrets and intellectual property, partnerships, real estate, employment, employee benefits, insurance, antitrust, and environmental regulation. Many clients choose to integrate the firm's lawyers into their business teams, where they serve as counselors,

Client projects often involve several practice areas. Pictured above are Lesley Moore, certified specialist in estate planning and probate law, and Allen Grumbine, coordinator of the firm's employee benefits practice.

strategists, and advisors in major corporate decisions. In addition to this focus on business, the firm has an extensive practice relating to the needs of individuals, ranging from estate planning to residential real estate closings.

The firm conducts its statewide practice from offices that overlook the historic and scenic Reedy River Falls in the heart of downtown Greenville. Its link to worldwide legal expertise is through membership in Lex Mundi, a global association of independent law firms. As the only Lex Mundi firm in South Carolina, Wyche attorneys can provide their clients with the benefits of an international legal referral network.

The common bond among the firm's attorneys is not only the practice of law, but also an abiding belief that each individual can and should make a difference in the community. Members of the firm have been actively involved in many major projects that have enhanced the quality of life in Greenville. The firm's attorneys have played vital roles in the creation and funding of the $36 million Peace Center for the Performing Arts, and have been

With offices overlooking the historic Reedy River Falls, the firm's spectacular scenic views are actually in the midst of a thriving downtown redevelopment district.

associated with almost every major initiative in the redevelopment of downtown Greenville, including the Hyatt Hotel, the historic West End, and the BI-LO Center arena. The firm's lawyers have assumed leadership roles with, and provided major support for, the Greenville Chamber of Commerce, the Greenville Symphony Association, the Community Foundation of Greater Greenville, the Greenville County Museum of Art, the Roper Mountain Science Center, the United Way, the YMCA, and many other organizations.

Additional information about the firm, including attorney profiles, personal e-mail addresses, a detailed description of practice areas, and a list of practice coordinators can be found on the Wyche, Burgess, Freeman & Parham home page at www.wyche.com.

Fluor Daniel

Fluor Daniel was founded from the strengths of Fluor Corporation and Daniel International, two of the most prestigious organizations in engineering and construction. Fluor purchased Daniel in 1977; however, the companies operated as distinct entities for nine years before merging into one dynamic, global company in 1986. Prior to being acquired by Fluor, Daniel International had based its operations in Greenville since 1942 after moving from Anderson, South Carolina, where the company started in 1934.

Fluor Daniel volunteers pose in front of a 1,000 square foot home they constructed for Habitat for Humanity in Greenville. (Photo by Jim Domnitz, Studio D Photographers.)

Today, Fluor Daniel serves more clients in more industries and more locations than any other company involved in providing engineering, construction, maintenance, and diversified services. With more than 60 electronically networked offices, Fluor Daniel supports projects in more than 80 countries located in the Americas, Europe, Africa, the Middle East, and the Asia Pacific region.

Fluor Daniel professionals design, engineer, and build a myriad of projects, which range from one-person assignments to jobs requiring thousands of engineers, specialists, and craft workers.

Going beyond the focus of customary engineering and construction, the mission of Fluor Daniel employees is to assist clients in attaining a competitive advantage by delivering services of unmatched value. These services include feasibility studies, site selection, conceptual design, project financing, technical services, project management, engineering, procurement, construction, equipment fleet management, plant operations, maintenance, and environmental services.

As for safety, Fluor Daniel employees are its most valuable asset, and the company virtually sets the global standard for safety practices. With a lost workday case incidence rate of .08 per 200,000 hours worked, Fluor Daniel is the world's safest contractor, with a safety performance 84 times better than the national industry average.

In Greenville, Fluor Daniel employs more than 2,500 workers. More than 70 percent are employed as professional, technical, or skilled workers, including engineers, administrators, sales and marketing professionals, and project managers.

The range of industries served by the Greenville operations center includes industrial, government, environmental, telecommunications, energy and chemicals, as well as diversified services including equipment sales and rental services, maintenance, and staffing services.

Fluor Daniel clients are served through flexible and highly responsive customer solution teams which bring the latest technologies, business solutions, and innovations to project needs.

Traditionally, the Fluor Daniel family of employees has donated its time, money, and efforts to support the needs of the Greenville community. Locally, the company is the largest contributor to the United Way's annual Fall pledge campaign.

Year in and year out, Fluor Daniel employees are involved in diverse volunteer activities. Many serve as tutors, board members, committee team members, while others offer helping hands for housing, beautification, community relief programs, and other charitable functions.

Fluor Daniel is an ardent supporter

Fluor Daniel's Greenville location is one of over 60 offices worldwide. (Photo by Jim Domnitz, Studio D Photographers.)

of education and the arts including the Greenville Zoo, the Roper Mountain Science Center, the Peace Center for the Performing Arts, the local library and museum, as well as the Greenville Symphony. Employees of Fluor Daniel plan, sponsor, and run Golf for Greenville, an annual charity golf tournament, which supports a selected local charity.

Whether it's delivering what clients need in a manner that's better, faster, cheaper, and safer than any other competitor, or organizing charitable events in the community, Fluor Daniel has taken the lead here at home in Greenville and throughout the world. ◖◗

227

Fluor Daniel provided construction management services for the BI-LO Center, shown here under construction in downtown Greenville. (Photo by Jim Domnitz, Studio D Photographers.)

Haynsworth Baldwin Johnson & Greaves LLC

The law firm of Haynsworth Baldwin Johnson & Greaves LLC does not strive to be all things to all people. Instead, the firm focuses on a few specialized areas of the law and provides its clients with practical and innovative strategies and solutions tailored to their individual needs.

Knox L. Haynsworth, Jr. founded the firm in 1972 for the purpose of representing management in the areas of labor, employment, and environmental law. More than 25 years later, the firm continues this tradition of specialization, having added the areas of workers' compensation, benefits, occupational safety and health, and immigration. With its headquarters in Greenville, the firm has eight offices in four states, and on any given day, its lawyers assist clients located throughout the United States. Many of the firm's clients are Fortune 500 companies, while others range from small local businesses to multinational corporations. The firm also represents public sector employers.

Haynsworth Baldwin Johnson & Greaves works closely with its clients to build harmonious employer/employee relationships that are based on cooperation and mutual respect and stresses proactive measures to prevent legal disputes. To help clients avoid employment-related problems, the firm conducts training programs and seminars on subjects such as employment discrimination, sexual harassment, immigration compliance, and violence in the workplace. The firm continuously monitors developing legal trends and, through newsletters and bulletins, alerts clients to new legal developments.

The firm has a national reputation for aggressively representing the interests of management when faced with employment and labor disputes. In recent years, it has represented clients before the United States Supreme Court in several important employment and labor cases. One case, *Gilmer v. Interstate/Johnson Lane Corp.*, resulted in a landmark decision upholding the enforceability of an employee's agreement to arbitrate a discrimination claim.

The firm is also nationally known for its success in helping companies stay union-free. Since 1972, it has handled more than 600 union election petitions before the National Labor Relations Board, and its clients have prevailed more than 95 percent of the time.

Members of the firm strongly believe that professional responsibility includes public and community service. Knox Haynsworth served as president of the South Carolina Bar Association from 1983 to 1984 and as president of the Greenville Bar Association in 1988. He is also a permanent member of the Fourth Circuit Judicial Conference, which covers the states of South Carolina, North Carolina, Virginia, West Virginia, and Maryland. Other members of the firm have engaged in a wide range of public and community service, which includes membership on charitable boards and committees of the state and local bar as well as leadership roles in various other organizations.

Greenville has been a perfect fit for the law firm throughout the years. Just as the city's economic growth, friendly people, and access to recreation and the arts make it an attractive location for new businesses, Greenville has also been an asset to the firm in attracting outstanding attorneys.

Throughout the years, Haynsworth Baldwin Johnson & Greaves has maintained long-term relationships with a substantial number of clients in Greenville, the Upstate, and throughout the nation. As it looks to the future, the firm plans to grow according to its clients' needs while maintaining its commitment to provide its clients with legal representation of the highest quality at a reasonable cost. ◪

228

Haynsworth law firm's home office in Greenville, South Carolina.

Phillips International, Inc.®

Phillips International, Inc.®, one of the larger executive search firms in South Carolina, was founded in Greenville during the recession in 1982 by Walter L. Phillips, Jr., CPC, its President. The

Walter L. Phillips, CPC, President of Phillips International.

company began by serving the apparel manufacturing industry where Walter Phillips was no stranger, having been the third generation of his family in apparel industry management. He resigned as Vice President of Corporate Operations of a large apparel company to pursue his interest in the executive search business after having served in apparel industry management with two companies for nearly 20 years.

Phillips International became well established as a leading search firm, locating mid to upper management candidates for client companies in the apparel industry during the mid 1980s. Soon it expanded into the textile and information technology industries. It continued to expand into environmental and financial search, and later into the areas of sales and manufacturing of industrial automation equipment and the packaging industry.

Today, Phillips has served more than 2,000 customers and has tens of thousands of candidate contacts worldwide from here to Hong Kong.

Keeping Abreast of Industry Changes

After NAFTA legislation passed, Mexico increasingly became a hot spot for American manufacturers. Phillips responded by adding a Mexican search consultant to better serve its client companies that were adding manufacturing there.

With the advent of the Internet and the World Wide Web, almost instant global communications became a reality, so Phillips International set up its own web page in 1996 through AT&T. This provided another medium of presenting its search services to companies around the globe. The company web page can be seen at www.phillipsintl.com.

Certification & Innovation

Walter Phillips says to his customers, "Our goal is to earn your repeat business," and this he does by becoming strategic partners and helping clients solve organizational problems through a high-quality professional search for the right person to fix their problems. The majority of Phillips' search consultants are CPCs (Certified Personnel Consultants). To become a CPC, one serves a two-year apprenticeship while studying employment law before taking the National CPC Exam.

Phillips International's success comes partly from its own unique, internally-developed system of operation for its search consultants. It consists of the CISM (Computer Integrated Search Management) system for the instant management of company and candidate data and its Time Block Planner, used for effective strategy and daily planning. Eighteen of its own professionally-edited videotapes and 400 pages of text form its own Objectives-Based Learning System for

keeping the team of search consultants on top. The results rank Phillips International, Inc.® in the top 10 percent in the U.S.

National Awards for Industry Leadership

In 1996, Phillips International, Inc.® won the Company Excellence Award for Commitment to the Industry from the National Association of Personnel Services (NAPS).

Walter Phillips serves on the Board of Directors of the South Carolina Association of Personnel Services and was its President in 1996. In November 1997, at the National Conference of NAPS in Dallas, he received the National Hall of Fame Award which states, "In recognition of leadership, innovation, and ability to take risks. Through personal conviction and actions he has improved the industry for all." This was the first time such an honor has been bestowed upon a South Carolina member.

In the final analysis, Phillips says, "it is the quality and dedication of the search consultants, the administrative staff, and the Greenville environment that have really made the company a success."

229

Phillips International's web page was established in 1996 to provide another medium of presenting their search services to companies worldwide.

Hardaway Law Firm, P.A.

*I*nnovations are the foundation of every business, ensuring its growth and survival. The research, developments, and marketing efforts of a company represent valuable assets to that business. Protecting these assets requires a thorough knowledge of Intellectual Property law. The attorneys of the Hardaway Law Firm, P.A. provide the expertise to help businesses make informed decisions with respect to patents, trademarks, copyrights, trade secrets, and technology transfer transactions.

The nature of the intellectual property assets of a business is unique, and their protection necessitates integrated and careful planning as a part of an ongoing business strategy. This approach ensures that U.S. and international patent applications can be timely filed, safeguards can be put in place to realize the full potential of trademarks and copyrights, and sensitive business plans and trade secrets can be maintained as confidential.

The Hardaway Law Firm, P.A. works to develop an integrated approach which is suitable to the unique character of a particular business, in order to identify and protect existing and future intellectual property assets. The firm advises businesses in implementing employment agreements and conducting workshops regarding intellectual property issues; helps implement confidentiality agreements and safeguards with customers and vendors to protect sensitive business

information; takes affirmative steps to achieve protection through patents, trademarks, and copyrights; and provides guidance in how to avoid infringing the intellectual property rights of others.

Recently, attorneys at Hardaway Law Firm completed a transaction for a multinational business whereby trademark rights had been acquired from predecessors-in-interest, including several Fortune 500 companies. The rights had originally been developed by a small business many years earlier. The multiple property transfers between the businesses, however, had failed to recognize the unique nature of intellectual property and proceeded to transfer trademark assets in the same way as tangible properties. As a result, legal title to the trademark had been jeopardized.

The Hardaway Law Firm worked with the business client and various companies located in multiple countries to reconstruct and legally perfect title in the trademark through the lineage of prior corporate entities. This effort included working within the specific confines of the national law of various foreign countries and resurrecting dissolved corporations.

Businesses receiving informed counsel on intellectual property assets early in their developing stages can be assured of the propriety of their holdings and can avoid potential calamities during corporate business transactions. The Hardaway Law Firm offers the required expertise, both to

the newly formed business, and to the business which suddenly discovers that the property it has acquired through prior transfers may not include certain major assets—the intellectual property.

It has always been an objective of the firm to foster close working relationships with those it serves. Its philosophy is to understand the client's marketing interests and requirements so that the efforts of the firm are consistent with the objectives of the client in tailoring an effective intellectual property strategy.

Founded in 1980, the firm represents clients' interests before the U.S. Patent and Trademark Office, the various U.S. court systems, and patent and trademark offices throughout the world via an international network of associate firms. In addition, Hardaway Law Firm acts as legal counsel to many foreign-based firms seeking representation of foreign clients in the U.S. Currently the firm represents, through associate council, clients from major European and Asian countries, including Russia, Japan, Germany, Italy, and Great Britain.

Attorneys in the firm include former examiners with the U.S. Patent and Trademark Office and accomplished international practitioners. Their academic concentrations cover a wide variety of technical and scientific fields and represent experience in private, corporate, and government settings.

State-of-the-art case management and docketing systems, as well as up-to-date technology for internet and web transactions, are a hallmark of the firm's commitment to provide the best available technical resources in service to clients.

Strongly tied to the community through professional, civic, and charitable organizations, the attorneys and legal staff at the Hardaway Law Firm contribute their time and efforts in promoting a high quality of life for the Greenville community.

Attorneys at Hardaway Law Firm, P.A., assisted by support personnel, provide complete services in intellectual property law.

Leatherwood Walker Todd & Mann, P.C.

The history and expertise of the law firm of Leatherwood Walker Todd & Mann, P.C. can be traced from 1945 when Wesley Walker and Dennis Leatherwood formed a partnership. Since then, the firm has flourished into more than a half century of long-lasting relationships with clients.

Working with clients as partners, putting client needs first, and addressing those needs with all available resources has been the firm's key to success throughout the years. LWT&M's services include litigation, corporate and finance, tax, intellectual property, real estate, construction, aviation, creditor's rights and bankruptcy, antitrust and trade regulation, employment law and workers' compensation, health law, insurance, criminal law, environmental law, as well as others. An LWT&M client enjoys the benefits of immediate access to the superior talents and experience of the entire LWT&M team. By taking a proactive approach, LWT&M strives to anticipate client needs, informing clients of significant changes and developments in the law which could affect their businesses.

From offices in Greenville and

The library at Leatherwood Walker Todd & Mann, P.C. is a two-story architectural focal point.

Spartanburg, LWT&M attorneys practice throughout South Carolina, focusing primarily on the Upstate. LWT&M's client base includes multinational organizations, regional companies, small businesses, manufacturers, general contractors, financial institutions, high-tech corporations, and insurance companies.

By design, most LWT&M attorneys join the firm immediately upon their graduation from law school. By mentoring young attorneys from the beginning of their careers, Leatherwood Walker Todd & Mann, P.C. has built a solid reputation as an ethical, highly-skilled, and responsible law firm offering tangible value to its clients.

To continually evaluate its own performance, LWT&M periodically seeks client comments, criticisms, and evaluation of the firm's legal services. This practice has helped LWT&M ensure that the qualities which built the firm's reputation and enhance its value are maintained.

LWT&M attorneys enjoy a close relationship with their community, becoming

(left to right) David A. Quattlebaum, III, J. Brantley Phillips, Jr., Harvey G. Sanders, Jr., James H. Watson, John E. Johnston, Jr., all of Leatherwood Walker Todd & Mann, P.C.

actively involved in its civic and charitable life. Local organizations benefiting from LWT&M involvement include the United Way, the Charles Aiken Academy, the Home for New Beginnings, the American Red Cross, the Palmetto Boys Shelter, and innumerable others.

The future of upstate South Carolina is bright. Leatherwood Walker Todd & Mann, P.C. is proud to be a member of the vibrant business community it serves and commits to continued quality, service, and value. ◙

Marshall Clarke Architects, Inc.

Conducting business the old-fashioned way. At Marshall Clarke Architects, Inc., practicing architecture is about much more than making a living—it's about quality design, public trust, making friends, and building lasting relationships.

Since its founding in 1976 by Marshall Clarke, FAIA, the firm has built its business on successfully establishing relationships beyond completion of the projects at hand. The vision established by the owner, architect, and contractor is reflected in all of the firm's projects.

A major factor in the Greenville-based firm's success has been adhering to the philosophy of listening and then providing responsive, high-quality designs to its clients, the public, and other design professionals. That philosophy has served the firm well in Greenville, as well as across the state and throughout the Southeast.

"In this business, you have to have confidence in the client and the client has to have confidence in you," says Marshall Clarke.

Long-term relationships have flourished through mutual confidence between the firm and its impressive list of clients. Names on the firm's client roster include BellSouth, Clemson University, Duke Power, BI-LO, the City of Greenville, Shriners Hospital, Michelin, Lockheed Martin, Springs Industries, and many

others. A number of the firm's clients have been confident in Marshall Clarke Architects' abilities and have continued their relationships for 10 to 20 years.

Through the years, Marshall Clarke Architects, Inc. has grown from a sole-proprietorship to more than 25 dedicated professionals. The firm is owned and managed by four principals— Marshall Clarke, FAIA; Jason Smith, AIA; Keith Clarke, AIA; and Michael Pry, AIA.

The firm prides itself on its ability to handle all aspects of the design process. "We are able to handle all of the design needs of our clients and manage the process from beginning to end," Clarke says.

Marshall Clarke Architects, Inc. offers professional services in the areas of architecture, planning and interior design, as well as environmental consulting. Its clients are involved in industrial, commercial office and retail, educational, institutional, religious, restaurant, assisted living, historic preservation, and environmental work.

To assure projects are completed to each client's expectations, a principal of the firm and a project architect are assigned for the

The renovation of Aldersgate United Methodist Church in Greenville, SC included a two-story education wing, a fellowship hall/kitchen, and additional classrooms.

duration of the job. This is just another way Marshall Clarke Architects, Inc. strives to be the best.

Going beyond conventional practice and serving the communities in which the firm provides services, accentuates the true spirit of the firm. Whether it's joining professional associations, Chambers of Commerce, or civic and service organizations, the professionals at Marshall Clarke Architects, Inc. focus on the issues affecting a community and actively commit time and energy to making a difference.

As the firm moves into the future, its business plan seeks opportunities to expand the business beyond the southeastern states. However, with a high percentage of its business coming from repeat clients, the firm knows its real future lies in listening and then providing responsive, high-quality designs that truly solve its clients' special needs. ◙

Marshall Clarke Architects, Inc. was selected to design a new North American headquarters, manufacturing, and service facility in Spartanburg, SC for Erhardt + Leimer, Inc., a German-owned company.

Love, Thornton, Arnold & Thomason, P.A.

"When I was a young loan officer, American Federal Bank (then Fidelity Federal) was represented by Love, Thornton, Arnold & Thomason. Today, after phenomenal growth and several mergers, American Federal is still represented by Love, Thornton, Arnold & Thomason. Why? Because of the firm's continuing commitment to be a partner with us in solving situations which arise on a daily basis. The firm's willingness to be a true advisor combined with its commitment to integrity and service to clients, are the reasons for this long-standing relationship." These are the words of American Federal Bank chairman emeritus Bill Merritt. His words could be those of any number of clients the firm serves in Greenville and throughout the Southeast.

James L. Love founded the firm in 1918, when Greenville was a small upstate town just beginning to blossom. Today, with Greenville firmly entrenched as a national and international center of business, the practice of law at Love, Thornton, Arnold & Thomason continues to evolve and grow along with the needs of its clients. The firm's diverse clientele includes banks, real estate developers and investors, construction companies, automobile manufacturers, colleges, and universities. The needs of these varied clients have greatly increased the areas of expertise held by members of the firm. Attorneys at Love, Thornton specialize and advise clients in an array of areas including banking, real estate, litigation, construction, corporate and business matters, environmental, land use, employment, workers' compensation, malpractice, insurance, and estate planning.

Love, Thornton is committed to "partnering" with its clients, which affords them the opportunity to openly and frankly express opinions and attitudes and to develop a true understanding of each other's needs. Often times, being a partner means helping clients anticipate issues before they become critical. "Competence is paramount, but equally valuable is trust and the ability to assess situations in the real world. That's why, even though we moved our corporate headquarters from Greenville to Madison, Georgia in 1992, we have continued to rely on the assistance of Love, Thornton for our development work all over the country," says Tom E. Dupree, Jr., Chairman and CEO of Apple South, Inc., a multi-concept restaurant company.

When litigation is necessary, the firm's attorneys vigorously represent their clients before all state and federal courts and administrative agencies. Love, Thornton's trial attorneys are noted for their skilled advocacy, as well as for their innovative trial techniques and problem solving abilities. Love, Thornton represents major casualty insurance carriers, as well as corporate and industrial clients in negligence, product liability, environmental, employment, and other civil and criminal litigation. Love, Thornton litigators have been elected to membership in the American College of Trial Lawyers, the American Board of Trial Advocates, and to the presidency of the South Carolina Defense Trial Attorneys Association.

Love, Thornton is known throughout South Carolina for not only its legal expertise and advocacy, but for the dedication of its members to the profession, the community, and the state. Love, Thornton attorneys regularly speak at continuing education programs, for other lawyers as well as for clients. Members of the firm have served on numerous boards, commissions, and charitable organizations locally and statewide, including the South Carolina House of Representatives, the State Ethics Commission, the Alliance for Quality Education, and the Greater Greenville Chamber of Commerce.

For 80 years, the attorneys of Love, Thornton, Arnold & Thomason have

For over 80 years, Love, Thornton, Arnold & Thomason has counseled business in Upstate South Carolina. Shown here is the firm's office in downtown Greenville. Photo by Russell Lowery.

233

served a dynamic and growing community. While the firm and the legal profession have changed over the years, Love, Thornton continues to hold fast to its heritage of credibility and integrity, along with the belief of practicing law in an ethical manner and treating each client's problem as its own are the keys to success.

Operations Associates

*I*n the Upstate's atmosphere of rapid business growth, Operations Associates—a firm of process-improvement engineers and system integrators—provides hands-on, targeted solutions for existing and relocating companies in the manufacturing and service industries.

The firm's professional team works side-by-side with industry leaders to implement progressive change, targeting solutions for specific problems. "We go beyond merely observing and detailing the problem—we implement action plans that remedy the problem. We're hands-on process improvement specialists," said John Auger, co-founder.

The Greenville-based company opened in 1993, and experiences a pattern of rapid growth. The firm's associates assume a hands-on approach to servicing clients in a multitude of categories, ranging from heavy industrial manufacturing to light service industries. "We implement programs that help clients achieve their goals—whether that's establishing a new state-of-the-art facility, or increasing performance in an existing business."

Auger, along with the company's other principals, Dave Miller, Mike Rigg, and Alan Nager, are focused process improvement engineers and systems integrators

that don't necessarily attempt to re-engineer an entire process, but rather focus on a specific client need. "We actively respond to the need and implement solutions. We work under defined timetables and budgets, and continually keep the client informed of progress," Auger said.

Operations Associates analyzes, designs, and implements targeted solutions in Supply Chain and Logistics Systems; Business Information Systems; Computer Systems Integration; Manufacturing, Warehouse, and Distribution Facilities; Material Handling Systems; Time Based Flow Strategies; Product Quality and Customer Service; Shop Floor Operations; and Human Resource Development. The firm provides services to many companies including Yamaha, Coca-Cola Bottling Company, Lockheed Martin, Capital One Financial, Ryobi, Hoffman LaRoche, Lucas Control Systems, and Spartanburg Stainless. Here's what a few clients have to say about their relationships with Operations Associates:

Sam Konduros, Alfmeier Corporation's Executive Vice President for North America, says "With less than 12 months until our first shipment of fuel management systems components was due at BMW, we were facing a tremendous challenge—to quickly build and start-up a plant that would live up to Alfmeier's proud European automotive heritage. Our goal was to meet the exacting requirements of our discriminating customers while accommodating our new American location, culture, and workforce. Operations Associates helped us pull together the resources to build and operate a world class facility from the inside out."

George Marshack of ICI Chemicals says

(left to right) Alfmeier Corporation Executive Vice President for North America Sam Konduros, Alfmeier President Markus Gebhardt, and Operations Associates co-founder John Auger meet on the grounds of Alfmeier's North American headquarters/manufacturing facility, developed using the "inside-out" planning services offered by Operations Associates.

"Operations Associates strong technical and interpersonal skills allowed us to migrate onto our new system in record time. They worked tirelessly, doing whatever was necessary to ensure our project's success. This type of commitment to excellence is often bantered about by consultants, but rarely demonstrated."

As a growing Upstate company, Operations Associates contributes positively to the community not only through business endeavors, but also through community involvement.

With more companies planning relocations to the Upstate and existing businesses continually searching for ways to enhance performance, Operations Associates offers a variety of services to meet the demands of area businesses.

Operations Associates looks forward to developing long-term relationships with clients, helping each business achieve maximum potential in the contemporary marketplace.

(left to right) Operations Associates co-founders Alan Nager, John Auger, Mike Rigg, and Dave Miller established the consulting firm in 1993, bringing operations and systems-based planners, engineers, and system integrators together to solve business challenges.

HOK Architects

E stablished in 1955 with a staff of just 26, Hellmuth Obata + Kassabaum has grown into the largest architectural and engineering firm in the world. Currently staffed with over 1,900 professionals, HOK has offices in 24 locations worldwide. HOK's South Carolina office (formerly CRSS Architects, Inc.) was originally part of the J.E. Sirrine Company, and has been practicing architecture in South Carolina since 1902.

HOK is unique. The firm's size and diversity enables HOK to provide design services for an array of project and client types at almost any site on the globe. In recent years, HOK's total gross billings have approached $1 million per week. In 1998, *World Architecture's* survey ranked HOK as the largest architectural practice, worldwide. *Engineering News Record's* 1997 survey of the top U.S. design firms ranked HOK as the top A/E firm in general building, and also in 1997, *Interior Design* ranked HOK as the fourth highest earner of interior design fees in the U.S.

From HOK's offices in Greenville, the firm's active principals Barbara M. Price, AIA; Michael P. Keeshen, AIA; James R. Fair, AIA; and Barry D. Jones, PE look out on an interesting and varied community. In alignment with the firm's core values, each HOK office is committed to making a

HOK's list of recent credits includes the Greenville County Courthouse Renovation and Judicial Wing Addition.

difference in the community in which it practices. For example, HOK regularly donates design services to the American Red Cross, most recently designing their new headquarters building also located in Greenville. Recognizing the important role that the Red Cross plays in the Upstate, HOK was honored to become partners with this agency in its endeavors to expand.

As part of HOK's quest for design excellence and social responsibility, the firm has cultivated a valued relationship with Clemson University. The principles routinely donate their time to teach classes and hold workshops. HOK maintains an internship program which provides architectural and engineering students with the opportunity to do a "hands-on" study of the design industry. In addition, each spring HOK sponsors the "HOK Design Excellence Award Program," which rewards architectural students for their senior design project with first place and honorable mention awards. HOK recognizes the importance of becoming directly involved in the lives of the aspiring young architects and engineers of the Upstate.

Architecture is multi-dimensional and incorporates a number of specialty fields such as master planning, interior design, graphics, site analysis, programming, and various kinds of engineering. Like few other professions, however, architecture tends to be a blend of dreamers and go-getters integrated with solid, team players. HOK, in particular, offers clients a wide spectrum of services, as well as a colorful group of professionals whose expertise is as varied as their backgrounds. HOK's staff includes not only architects, interior designers, planners, and

HOK's Greenville professionals provided architectural and engineering design services for the award winning James H. Woodside Conference Center. Pictured (left to right) are principals Barbara Price, Mike Keeshen, and Barry Jones.

engineers, but also consultants, specifications writers, programmers, construction managers, landscape architects, graphic specialists, delineators, and model builders.

HOK's core belief of integrating design excellence with client needs is based on its philosophy to create environments that go beyond pure function. The firm's goal is to create buildings that enhance the quality of life for those who live and work in them . . . to create buildings that satisfy the physical, emotional, and intellectual needs of each particular client. For this reason, there is no "HOK style." HOK approaches each project individually and without preconceptions. This philosophy, along with the firm's superior track record, ensures that HOK will continue to provide the best in architectural and engineering design services in South Carolina for decades to come. ◄

235

Studio D Photographers

Photography is an art which takes know-how and expertise, and that is what the professional team at Studio D Photographers has to offer. With more than 70 years of combined experience, Studio D presents clients with quality work that rates second to none.

Importantly, each of the three photographers on staff have advanced degrees in photography, and the team has won a host of photography awards from state and national associations as well as the Kodak Gallery and Fuji Masterpiece awards.

Studio D is a progressive, 5,000 square foot state-of-the-art operation with the latest in digital and conventional photography equipment. The new digital equipment allows for retouching and enhancement of images—perfect for product catalogs and tabletop photography.

The studio's growth—since Jim Domnitz began the operation in his garage in 1979—has followed the fast-track growth experience of Greenville during the past 20 years. Studio D clients include local and international corporations. General Electric, Michelin Tire, Dunlop

236

The photographers of Studio D will photograph for anyone, anywhere, anytime!

Maxfli Sports Corporation, Fluor Daniel, Hoechst Celanese, and Hitachi are only a few of the recognizable names that have retained Studio D's services.

Domnitz says he and his staff listen to their customers and client input is always welcome on all projects. Easy to work with, Studio D will accommodate a client's requests involving anything from shots of a difficult nature to extensive travel. Throughout the years, personal service, the adherence to deadlines, and unique imaginative images has established Studio D as the premiere photography studio in the region.

The studio's capabilities include, but are not limited to,

Studio D Photographers blend conventional photography with the technology of digital imaging.

architectural photography, in studio digital imaging of products, on location industrial environments, aerial photography and people photography for illustrative purposes, as well as news release business portraits.

While tending to business, Domnitz has maintained a Chamber involvement and is past president of the Greenville Chamber Northwest Area Council and a Leadership Greenville graduate. ⊡

Bibliography

Ashmore, Nancy Vance. *Greenville Woven from the Past*. Northridge, California: Windsor Publications, Inc. 1986.

Gould, Scott. *Greenville Coming of Age*. Memphis, Tennessee: Towery Publishing Inc. 1992.

Richardson, James M. *History of Greenville County South Carolina*. Atlanta, Georgia: A.H. Cawston. 1930.

Staff. *The 1997 Visitors and Newcomers Guide to Greenville*. South Carolina: Multimedia Publishing. 1997.

Enterprises Index

Index